Publisher's Foreword

Dear HowExpert Reader,

HowExpert publishes quick 'how to' guides on all topics from A to Z by everyday experts.

At HowExpert, our mission is to discover, empower, and maximize everyday people's talents to ultimately make a positive impact in the world for all topics from A to Z...one everyday expert at a time!

All of our HowExpert guides are written by everyday people just like you and me, who have a passion, knowledge, and expertise for a specific topic.

We take great pride in selecting everyday experts who have a passion, real-life experience in a topic, and excellent writing skills to teach you about the topic you are also passionate about and eager to learn.

We hope you get a lot of value from our HowExpert guides, and it can make a positive impact on your life in some way. All of our readers, including you, help us continue living our mission of positively impacting the world for all spheres of influences from A to Z.

If you enjoyed one of our HowExpert guides, then please take a moment to send us your feedback from wherever you got this book.

Thank you, and we wish you all the best in all aspects of life.

Sincerely,

BJ Min
Founder & Publisher of HowExpert
HowExpert.com

PS...If you are also interested in becoming a HowExpert author, then please visit our website at HowExpert.com/writers. Thank you & again, all the best!

COPYRIGHT, LEGAL NOTICE AND DISCLAIMER:

COPYRIGHT © BY HOWEXPERT™ (OWNED BY HOT METHODS). ALL RIGHTS RESERVED WORLDWIDE. NO PART OF THIS PUBLICATION MAY BE REPRODUCED IN ANY FORM OR BY ANY MEANS, INCLUDING SCANNING, PHOTOCOPYING, OR OTHERWISE WITHOUT PRIOR WRITTEN PERMISSION OF THE COPYRIGHT HOLDER.

DISCLAIMER AND TERMS OF USE: PLEASE NOTE THAT MUCH OF THIS PUBLICATION IS BASED ON PERSONAL EXPERIENCE AND ANECDOTAL EVIDENCE. ALTHOUGH THE AUTHOR AND PUBLISHER HAVE MADE EVERY REASONABLE ATTEMPT TO ACHIEVE COMPLETE ACCURACY OF THE CONTENT IN THIS GUIDE, THEY ASSUME NO RESPONSIBILITY FOR ERRORS OR OMISSIONS. ALSO, YOU SHOULD USE THIS INFORMATION AS YOU SEE FIT, AND AT YOUR OWN RISK. YOUR PARTICULAR SITUATION MAY NOT BE EXACTLY SUITED TO THE EXAMPLES ILLUSTRATED HERE; IN FACT, IT'S LIKELY THAT THEY WON'T BE THE SAME, AND YOU SHOULD ADJUST YOUR USE OF THE INFORMATION AND RECOMMENDATIONS ACCORDINGLY.

THE AUTHOR AND PUBLISHER DO NOT WARRANT THE PERFORMANCE, EFFECTIVENESS OR APPLICABILITY OF ANY SITES LISTED OR LINKED TO IN THIS BOOK. ALL LINKS ARE FOR INFORMATION PURPOSES ONLY AND ARE NOT WARRANTED FOR CONTENT, ACCURACY OR ANY OTHER IMPLIED OR EXPLICIT PURPOSE.

ANY TRADEMARKS, SERVICE MARKS, PRODUCT NAMES OR NAMED FEATURES ARE ASSUMED TO BE THE PROPERTY OF THEIR RESPECTIVE OWNERS, AND ARE USED ONLY FOR REFERENCE. THERE IS NO IMPLIED ENDORSEMENT IF WE USE ONE OF THESE TERMS.

NO PART OF THIS BOOK MAY BE REPRODUCED, STORED IN A RETRIEVAL SYSTEM, OR TRANSMITTED BY ANY OTHER MEANS: ELECTRONIC, MECHANICAL, PHOTOCOPYING, RECORDING, OR OTHERWISE, WITHOUT THE PRIOR WRITTEN PERMISSION OF THE AUTHOR.

ANY VIOLATION BY STEALING THIS BOOK OR DOWNLOADING OR SHARING IT ILLEGALLY WILL BE PROSECUTED BY LAWYERS TO THE FULLEST EXTENT. THIS PUBLICATION IS PROTECTED UNDER THE US COPYRIGHT ACT OF 1976 AND ALL OTHER APPLICABLE INTERNATIONAL, FEDERAL, STATE AND LOCAL LAWS AND ALL RIGHTS ARE RESERVED, INCLUDING RESALE RIGHTS: YOU ARE NOT ALLOWED TO GIVE OR SELL THIS GUIDE TO ANYONE ELSE.

THIS PUBLICATION IS DESIGNED TO PROVIDE ACCURATE AND AUTHORITATIVE INFORMATION WITH REGARD TO THE SUBJECT MATTER COVERED. IT IS SOLD WITH THE UNDERSTANDING THAT THE AUTHORS AND PUBLISHERS ARE NOT ENGAGED IN RENDERING LEGAL, FINANCIAL, OR OTHER PROFESSIONAL ADVICE. LAWS AND PRACTICES OFTEN VARY FROM STATE TO STATE AND IF LEGAL OR OTHER EXPERT ASSISTANCE IS REQUIRED, THE SERVICES OF A PROFESSIONAL SHOULD BE SOUGHT. THE AUTHORS AND PUBLISHER SPECIFICALLY DISCLAIM ANY LIABILITY THAT IS INCURRED FROM THE USE OR APPLICATION OF THE CONTENTS OF THIS BOOK.

COPYRIGHT BY HOWEXPERT™ (OWNED BY HOT METHODS)
ALL RIGHTS RESERVED WORLDWIDE.

HowExpert Guide to Craft Beer

101 Lessons to Learn the Facts, History, and Joy of Craft Beers from A to Z

HowExpert with Paul Deines

Copyright HowExpert™
www.HowExpert.com

For more tips related to this topic, visit HowExpert.com/craftbeer.

Recommended Resources

- HowExpert.com – Quick 'How To' Guides on All Topics from A to Z by Everyday Experts.
- HowExpert.com/free – Free HowExpert Email Newsletter.
- HowExpert.com/books – HowExpert Books
- HowExpert.com/courses – HowExpert Courses
- HowExpert.com/clothing – HowExpert Clothing
- HowExpert.com/membership – HowExpert Membership Site
- HowExpert.com/affiliates – HowExpert Affiliate Program
- HowExpert.com/jobs – HowExpert Jobs
- HowExpert.com/writers – Write About Your #1 Passion/Knowledge/Expertise & Become a HowExpert Author.
- HowExpert.com/resources – Additional HowExpert Recommended Resources
- YouTube.com/HowExpert – Subscribe to HowExpert YouTube.
- Instagram.com/HowExpert – Follow HowExpert on Instagram.
- Facebook.com/HowExpert – Follow HowExpert on Facebook.

Table of Contents

Recommended Resources 2

Publisher's Foreword.. 3

Chapter 1: Approaching the Unruly World of Craft Beer 6

Chapter 2: What You Should Know About the History of Beer 17

Chapter 3: Understanding Beer Styles and Traditions 29

Chapter 4: The Modern American Craft Beer Movement... 45

Chapter 5: How to Approach a Taproom 60

Chapter 6: Knowing Your Metrics............................. 69

Chapter 7: Knowing the Variables..............................81

Chapter 8: Navigating the Craft Beer Hype Train 98

Top 10 Popular Craft Beers for Beginners 109

Frequently Asked Questions 114

About the Expert 120

Recommended Resources 121

Chapter 1: Approaching the Unruly World of Craft Beer

The craft beer world can seem vast and impenetrable. There are so many breweries, so many types of beer, so much history, and so many points of entry. It's no wonder people wave away the whole thing and say, "I'm not a beer drinker."

Yet there's a world of innovative, enticing, invigorating ales and lagers out there. Even if you don't consider yourself a beer person, is there something out there you might like? Where do you start?

It's not surprising that so many people get turned off by beer early on. Our introduction to beer so often comes in the form of a Bud Light handed to us at a party. If a fizzy, vaguely bitter, somewhat grainy yellow drink isn't to your taste, you might have decided to stick with more exciting, flavorful options like wine or cocktails. That makes sense!

The good news, if you've decided to see what this whole craft beer scene is about, is that you are about to enter a world of robust, innovative, tasty potables that will make you forget all about that tepid Bud.

So, let's start by charting our point of approach for craft beer.

Lesson 1: Think About Other Things You Like to Drink.

There are a lot of different beers out there. The bad news is that it can be intimidating for someone new to the scene. But that's also good news! Today, beer is so varied and is evolving at such a fast pace that you can be guaranteed to find something to your taste. Are you a Merlot drinker? Try Deschutes Brewing's Mirror Mirror, a dark Strong Ale aged in red wine casks. Like whiskey? Try one of the FiftyFifty Brewing Eclipse Stouts, which are conditioned in different bourbon barrels. Grimm Artisanal Ales has a series of tart, light Berliner Weisse-style beers that incorporate vanilla bean and fruits, perfect for a cream soda lover. There is a beer out there for every taste right now. You just have to familiarize yourself with the options.

Lesson 2: Are Ales and Lagers Different Things?

You can think of Ales and Lagers as the two families of beer. Pretty much every "beer style" falls into one of these two camps. The difference has to do with how each family is fermented. Yeast is the mechanism by which unfermented beer, or wort, becomes alcoholic beer. Ales use top-fermenting yeast, which does its work in higher temperatures; stouts, Porters, Barleywines, IPAs, and Lambics are all ales. Conversely, Lagers use bottom-fermenting yeast, which requires lower temperatures. Lagers tend to be (but aren't always) lighter and crisper.

Lesson 3: What is a Beer Style?

First, let's take a moment to discuss, in broad terms, how you brew beer. You start by steeping malted grain in hot water, kind of like you're making a bread tea. Then you boil the resulting sugary concoction with hops, a plant that imparts bitterness and some flavors. Finally, you pitch in the aforementioned yeast and let the whole thing ferment over the coming weeks. This yeast also creates carbon dioxide, which gives the beer its natural effervescence.

Knowing this process, we can now discuss how variations in each of its steps and ingredients can create different "styles" of beers. For example:

Malts

Depending on the malted grain you use, you can change the taste, smell, color, and consistency of the resulting beverage. Lagers and Pale Ales often use Pilsner and 2-Row malts. Stouts use Munich, Black, and Chocolate malts, as well as roasted barley, for a darker hue and fuller taste. Wheat beers, unsurprisingly, incorporate wheat in the malt bill. The more malted grain you use, the more sugar is produced, and the more alcohol is converted by the yeast. So, huge boozy ales, like Barleywines or Belgian Quads, have large malt bills.

Hops

As stated before, hops impart bitterness and flavor. Their presence is especially prominent in IPAs. When you add them early in the boil, they make the resulting beer more bitter. When you add them later, or "dry-hop" during fermentation, they will produce more fruity, earthy flavors and less raw bitterness. In more malt-focused beers, hops are less pronounced. For example, sweet Belgian Abbey beers often use aged hop plants, which impart more muted spice and herbal notes.

Yeast

Yeast produces alcohol and carbonation, but it also contributes a lot of flavors. Certain yeasts are endemic to specific styles. For example, Farmhouse Ales use a yeast strain that converts - or attenuates - a lot of sugar and imparts spicy and estery notes. Wild ales - like Belgian Lambic - often use airborne cultures that create a funky, sour character.

These are just a few examples of how the brewing process produces different "styles" of beer. Bear in mind, while styles are officially regulated in beer competitions, they can be more amorphous in the real world. Most beers hew to a given style, but many straddle lines and play with conventions. So, don't be surprised if you come across a Blond Stout or a Sour IPA. That's all part of the weird fun!

Lesson 4: With So Many Styles Out There, Don't Be Afraid to Pick and Choose.

Bearing in mind what was discussed above, don't fret about liking the beer that beer nerds tell you is the best. If IPAs are too bitter for your palate right now, skip them. They aren't going anywhere! The same goes for that 17% ABV Barrel-Aged Pastry Stout everyone is raving about at the bar. If you like big, chocolaty beers that make your vision go a little blurry, go for it! Otherwise, there are plenty of lighter, more delicate brews to select instead.

Lesson 5: Get Acquainted with Your Local Options

Today, there are over eight thousand breweries in the United States. California has the most, with nearly one thousand. Per capita, Vermont has the highest concentration of breweries. Wherever you live in this country, you probably have a brewery within a short driving distance. It's always a great idea to start locally when you're becoming acquainted with craft beer.

For one thing, most beer tastes best fresh, and your local beer maker will have the freshest product. You will also have access to their new and limited releases. And who knows? You might be living near the next super-hyped brewery!

Lesson 6: Top-Rated Breweries are Not Relegated to One Area of the Country!

The website RateBeer's 2020 top-10 rated breweries included nine US craft brewers. They are located in New England, the Midwest, the South, and the West Coast. Only one is located in a US city with a top-10 population: AleSmith Brewing in San Diego. The other eight are located in mid-size markets. The top-rated brewer in America, Hill Farmstead Brewery, operates out of Greensboro, Vermont, with a population of 762 people. It goes to prove that you don't need to live in a major metropolis or a hyper-specific area of the country to have access to world-class beer!

Lesson 7: Get to Know Your Local Bartenders, Beer-Tenders, and Bottle Sellers

Do you know who knows a lot about beer? Beer professionals. Heck, they may even know more than I do! Folks that brew, pour, and sell craft beer have as wide a breadth of knowledge as one can imagine. Place yourself in their hands, and they will steer you well. They can tailor their recommendations to your preferences and offer some context for the dizzying options out there. And being someone's beer resource is a privilege for most of them. You could liken it to a record store employee - back when such things existed - pressing a favorite band's album into a customer's hands. Find a local taproom worker, bottle shop worker, or bartender that you trust, and you will never want for good beer intel.

Lesson 8: Beer Is a Drink to be Paired! Think of It as a Menu Item.

One of the roadblocks to starting with craft beer is approaching it as a goal unto itself. Many first-timers look at shelf upon shelf of strange ales with wacky labels and in-joke names and wonder *which one will taste good*. A more productive and less rage-inducing question might be, *which one will taste best with tonight's dinner*. Simple as this might sound, it can make all the difference. Rather than looking for some undefinable "good beer," think about what might work with that steak you're making tonight. Personally, I love choosing a good Saison-style ale to pair with Thanksgiving dinner: a farmhouse beer for a farmhouse meal that really pulls the dining experience together. Ever do breakfast for dinner? Why not pour a huge coffee-infused Breakfast Stout to go with those nighttime pancakes and bacon? Thinking about beer pairings might also compel you to drink styles that you wouldn't otherwise try.

Lesson 9: Some Beers are Refreshing, Some are Night-Enders. Think about Which Beers Fit Which Events.

Would you drink a big glass of Cabernet by a pool in hundred-degree weather? What about a frosty cool gin-and-tonic in front of a fire on a winter night? There's nothing wrong with doing either of those choices. However, some drinks pair best with certain situations. The same is true for beer. So, think of your craft beers as accompaniments to your day. A fruit-fermented Sour would be great for that poolside afternoon, and a Barrel-Aged Wheatwine would warm you up on a snowy night.

Lesson 10: Knowing the Difference Between Craft and "Crafty"

Remember, once upon a time, when there were three beer options out there, and they all looked and tasted virtually the same? As you can imagine, the rise in craft beer's popularity has eaten into the market share of macro-beer conglomerates like AB-InBev or MolsonCoors. In 2019, craft brewers - as defined by the Brewer's Association - represented 13.6% of the US beer market, compared to 7.9% a decade earlier. That growth comes at the expense of the big boys. How have they responded? In addition to a flurry of ads meant to paint craft beer drinkers to effete snobs (see: Budweiser's *dilly-dilly* campaign), they have tried building inroads into the craft market with a series of "crafty" options:

Crafty Labels from Macro Conglomerates

Ask somebody what their favorite craft beer is, and you might hear Blue Moon, Steel Reserve, or LandShark. These labels were actually all developed and produced by the big three American brands. The first is a Coors beer, the second comes from Miller, and the last is a Budweiser brand.

Craft Breweries acquired by Macro Conglomerates.

The big three macro-brewers have been on a bit of a shopping spree over the last decade. What they're buying are craft brewers. The highest-profile of these is Anheuser Busch's "High End" stable. This group of acquisitions includes Blue Point, 10 Barrel, Elysian, Golden Road, Breckenridge, and - the jewel in their crown - Goose Island.

There's nothing inherently inferior about "crafty" beers. Blue Moon, for example, is an excellent example of the traditional Witbier. Goose Island's annual Bourbon County Brand release is still one of the year's hallmark beer events. Additionally, you can't argue that a payday from a big brewer is a worthwhile reward for craft owners that struggled in a low-margin business for a long time. However, drinkers should be aware that these acquired brands are part of a production and distribution Goliath. You often see Blue Point Toasted Lager and Goose Island 312 on the same tap list or grocery shelf as Bud Light because AB-InBev uses its distribution pipeline to force out independent craft brands.

Luckily, beer drinkers have an easy way to know if a beer is craft or crafty. The Brewer's Association has a seal for independent brands. It appears on all bottles, cans, and packaging. If you don't see the seal, there's a decent shot the product is crafty. You can find information on the BA seal at https://www.brewersassociation.org/independent-craft-brewer-seal/.

Lesson 11: This Shouldn't Be Work! Find Pals to Take the Journey with You.

Finally, there's no reason to take this trip alone. Exploring the wild, bustling world of craft beer is improved by having someone to share the ride. See if your significant other wants to join the fun, so you can choose a growler of local ale to pair with your dinner. Rope in some buddies and incorporate zany brews into your game day spread. What about opening a 750ML bottle of stout on movie night? Trivia night at a craft-centric gastropub? The whole idea is to make this a social endeavor because beer is now and has always been a social drink. Prost!

It's reasonable to be wary of the craft beer world. The selection can be harrowing, the terminology confusing, and, candidly, the community can be pretty insular. But that does not mean that beer-lovers want to lock the doors on new arrivals. On the contrary, there's nothing quite as invigorating for a beer nerd as introducing someone to a beer that opens their eyes and their palate. I can attest to this personally.

Chapter Review

I hope this will be an exciting journey for you and that you don't feel undue pressure. To recap:

- When figuring out what beer you might like, think about other drinks you enjoy. Some beers draw from the flavor profiles of wine, spirits, soda, milkshakes, and more!
- Start local – you probably have a brewery near you, and it can provide you with the freshest product around.

- Draw from the knowledge of beer servers and beer sellers. They want to help you find your new favorite beverage!
- Feel free to pick and choose. You will prefer certain styles over others, so explore be drink what you like.
- Make this process fun. Have friends and family join you. Make craft beer part of your recreational framework, pairing particular brews with particular meals and events.

My goal is to get you excited, impart some knowledge, and demystify this unruly world of craft beer. I'm confident that the chapters that follow will pique your interest and make you thirsty.

So, let's get moving. There's a lot to cover.

Chapter 2: What You Should Know About the History of Beer

Before we dive headlong into the contemporary craft beer scene, it's worth having a little primer on the history of beer.

Don't worry! I promise that this will not turn into a high school history class. I simply want to place our current beer community in the context of a larger historical arc. After all, today's brewers are in constant communication with historical traditions.

Rest assured, this will be fun and breezy. Plus, you're about to pick up some fun factoids that will impress the other folks in the taproom.

Lesson 12: It's Not an Exaggeration to Say that the History of Beer is the History of Human Civilization

To a large extent, beer is the inevitable product of the human transition from hunting and gathering to a settled agrarian lifestyle. For reference, that transition happened about 12,000 years ago; around 7000 BCE, the first known fermented beverage emerged in China, a rice-and-honey drink. Fermentation was more than just a way to have a good time. It was a means of survival. Before water purification and filtration, fostering ethanol in water was the best way to make it potable.

Lesson 13: Some of the Earliest-Known Beverages Are Beer

People consumed specially-brewed grain- and barley-based alcoholic drinks as part of religious rites and family events for centuries. If you visit the University of Pennsylvania Museum of Archaeology and Anthropology in Philadelphia, you can see ancient Sumerian drinking vessels that were used for drinking beer. Mesopotamian cylinder seals show images of people quaffing grain-based booze through reed straws. While drinking a beer through a straw might be gauche now, in the old days, it was the best way to enjoy a drink without ingesting lots of sediment. Researchers recently translated a five-thousand-year-old hymn to the Sumerian beer goddess Ninkasi on some tablets discovered in Iraq. Included in the poem is something of an ancient recipe. Here's an excerpt:

Ninkasi, you are the one who soaks the malt in a jar,

The waves rise, the waves fall.

...

You are the one who spreads the cooked mash on large reed mats,

Coolness overcomes,

...

You are the one who holds with both hands the great sweet wort,

Brewing [it] with honey [and] wine

By the way, there is a nice Oregon craft brewer called Ninkasi Brewing. As they say, everything old is new again.

Lesson 14: Check Out a Fantastic Ale Brewed from an Ancient Recipe

In 1957, the University of Pennsylvania Museum of Archaeology and Anthropology excavated a nearly three-thousand-year-old tomb in Turkey. They discovered a vessel that showed evidence of a liquid containing barley, honey, and grapes. A half-century later, Sam Calagione of Dogfish Head Brewing in Delaware partnered with biomolecular archaeologist Dr. Patrick McGovern of the Penn Museum to develop an ale inspired by this long-lost brew. The resulting beer, Midas Touch, exists in the three-way crossroad of ale, honey-mead, and white wine. Saffron subs in for hops, which had not been domesticated in the ancient world. Midas Touch a great entry-point beer if you're a chardonnay lover. It's also a multiple-award-winning ale, available year-round in pretty much every American city.

Lesson 15: People Brewed Beer Before They Even Knew How Fermentation Worked.

These early grain potables were fermented using "spontaneous" methods. That is to say; the wort was left out in uncovered vessels and converted to booze by exposure to micro-flora in the air. Traditional Lambics use the same technique, so if you want a sense of the funky, tart result, maybe check out modern Gueuzes from Belgian outfits like Drie Fonteinen or Boon. If you know your science history, you'll recall that yeast cultures were not properly discovered and cataloged until Louis Pasteur's work in the nineteenth century. So even well into the Medieval era, fermentation was a mystical process. Vikings, for example, kept a "beer stick" that would kickstart fermentation by exposing wort to its accumulated yeast microbes. Beer-brewing monks did their best to standardize fermentation by retaining a little sediment from each batch and pitching it into the next. What did they call this apparent magical culture? Godisgoode.

Lesson 16: Germany Codified What Beer Was in the Sixteenth Century

On April 23, 1516, the whole of Bavaria adopted a law limiting beer ingredients to water, barley, and hops. As mentioned above, they did not include yeast since it had not yet been identified. This law, called the Reinheitsgebot, eventually expanded to all of what is now called Germany. It's still on the books today. If you consider the types of beer most commonly associated with Germany - and Bavaria in particular - you can see the Reinheitsgebot's effect. There are, to be clear, countless exemplary beers from this region. Weihestephaner, Spaten, Ayinger, Aecht Schlenkerla - these are just a few German brewers that have made astonishing lagers that conform to the Reinheitsgebot.

Yet many fear that such adherence has made the community slow to embrace international trends and adapt.

Lesson 17: Check Out Some Old World beers that Thumbed Their Nose at the Reinheitsgebot

It's tempting to think of all Old World beers as a musty, undifferentiated affair. The honest-to-god truth is that many brewers were pushing the limits, even as the Reinheitsgebot controlled the beer brewed in Germany. Here are some examples of older beers you can try today that thumbed their nose at "beer purity:"

Belgian Gueuzes

Golden ales are fermented in long, open "cool ship" troughs, taking in the micro-organisms floating around, then aging for months, even years, in foeders. The different ales are blended into a funky, tart concoction called a Gueuze. Sometimes they are further aged with fruit to craft other variations: with raspberry, it's a Framboise, with cherries, a Kriek. The brewers and blenders of Brussels have been doing this for centuries. Some popular Gueuze producers are Boon, Lindeman's, Cantillon, and Tilquin.

Flanders Reds

Another fruity sour from Belgium, these dark ales ferment with diabolical, lactic-acid-producing yeast strains. Sometimes, brewers add fruit during fermentation. The resulting ales are thick-bodied, sour, and popping with stewed plum notes. Rodenbach is the quintessential example, one that's available in most stores.

English Milk Stouts

Today, you can find just about anything under the sun in your Stouts, from coffee to coconut to habaneros. The major innovation the English brought to their signature dark ale was lactose, the milk sugar that does not convert to alcohol when combined with brewer's yeast. Milk Stouts have a thick, velvety mouthfeel and easy-drinking sweetness. Some fantastic examples are Old Engine Oil from Harviestoun Brewery and Mackeson Triple XXX Stout from Whitbread.

The Berliner Weisse

Even in Germany itself, brewers colored outside the Reinheitsgebot boundaries. The Berliner Weisse is a light, sour wheat beer fermented with bacillus strains of yeast, creating the same lactic acid character of the Flanders sours. The resulting beer is tart and quite refreshing, often mixed with fruit after pouring. Craft brewers now add the fruit during fermentation. Napoleon's troops are said to have called the Berliner Weisse the "champagne of the north." Take that, Miller High Life! If you want to try a real old-school German Berliner Weisse, your best bet is probably the one brewed by Bayerischer Bahnhof.

Elsewhere...

Throughout Scandinavia, brewers incorporated local fruits and plants for centuries. In France, the Biere de Garde took on characteristics for the Belgian farmhouse ales across the border, sometimes incorporating wild yeast and adjunct ingredients. In Asia, rice was a common alternative to malt. Of course, many brewers today often use rice to booze alcohol without creating a heavier brew.

Lesson 18: Many of America's Founding Fathers made Beer and Cider

Many of the United States' founders were farmers as well as statesmen. As mentioned above, fermented beverages prevailed before water purification became common. As such, many of our Founding Fathers kept brewing systems in their homes for beer and cider production. Thomas Jefferson had such a setup in Monticello. The same is true of George Washington's Mount Vernon. Curators in Mount Vernon recently unearthed Washington's recipe for a low-alcohol "small beer." Washington's relationship with booze was multifaceted. He insisted that daily provisions for his Revolutionary War troops include a quart of beer. In his later years, Washington helped found a distillery, putting Mount Vernon's excess grain to use in whiskey production.

Contrary to popular assumptions, Samuel Adams was not a brewer. He and his father were maltsters, providing malted grain to brewers. Of course, he put this aside when he joined the fight for colonial independence.

Lesson 19: Have a Taste of an Eighteenth-Century Recipe in Virginia

You needn't invent the time machine to find out what a colonial brew tasted like. Those recipes are still brewed today. Alewerks in Williamsburg, Virginia, brews a Brown Ale called Old Stitch, using portions and ingredients common for the eighteenth century. Old Stitch was the first collaboration between Alewerks and the Historic Foodways program of Colonial Williamsburg. You can try it yourself when stopping into one of Colonial Williamsburg's pubs and restaurants. Alewerks went on to craft a colonial-style Porter and an Extra Special Bitter.

Lesson 20: Raise a Glass at the Founding Fathers' Tavern in New York

Remember early in the musical *Hamilton* when Alexander, Aaron Burr, Lafayette, and others gather in a tavern to drink and debate? There's a decent chance that the location is Fraunces Tavern in Lower Manhattan. Situated on 54 Pearl Street, the tavern opened in the 1760s under the management of Samuel Fraunces. A mainstay of the revolutionary elite, Fraunces Tavern hosted the Sons of Liberty on multiple occasions. After the British surrendered, George Washington hosted revolutionary troops there for a farewell meal. The Foreign Affairs, War, and

Finance departments were initially headquartered there. Today, the tavern is still a functioning restaurant - the oldest in New York - and museum. So, drop in, eat a good meal, and drink from a selection of craft beers.

Lesson 21: A Look at the American Beer Scene Before Prohibition

Any American coming of age between World War II and the nineties might think that three big brewers controlled the whole beer market since the first European ship anchored. The reality is much different. Before the Eighteenth Amendment outlawed the manufacture, transportation, and sale of alcohol in the United States, around four thousand breweries operated domestically. The type of beer produced reflected the eclectic melting-pot of immigrant cultures. The market had plenty of light Bohemian-style Lagers, but it also had Porters, Cream Ales, Steam Beers, and Bitters. Beer made its way to the masses primarily through saloons, meaning you either drank it there or carried it off in a growler. That's not so different from the setup in most small craft taprooms today!

Lesson 22: How Did Breweries Survive When Selling Beer Was Illegal?

Everything changed with Prohibition. Remember those four thousand breweries before the ban? After Prohibition's repeal, that number was thirty-one. Those brewers survived the ban by pivoting to other products, including malted milk, soda, and fruit juice. There were also near-beer products that rose and fell in popularity. Budweiser created a non-alcoholic malt drink call Bevo, which initially turned a profit but eventually tanked. Miller had a similar product called Vivo. Indeed, it helped that most of these brewers had real estate holdings that kept them afloat in the first years of Prohibition.

Many brewers happened upon the idea of selling the individual ingredients for beer-making: malt syrup, yeast, and hops. These products weren't illegal under Prohibition and were a boon to homebrewers and bootleggers alike.

Lesson 23: How Prohibition Changed the World of American Brewing for Decades.

Within a year of Prohibition's repeal, the number of brewers operating in the US grew to about nine-hundred. It would soon contract again, though. The tastes of American drinkers shifted during the ban. A population now accustomed to lighter non-alcoholic drinks wanted something closer to soda but with an alcoholic kick. Remember that first Bud Light you drank back in the day? That type of lager was the market correction that brewers undertook to meet demand. Czech Lagers, Pilsners, Kellerbiers, Helles - these became the beers of choice for American drinkers. As such, the operations of German immigrants like Adolph Coors and Adolphus Busch rose to the top. They produced a high-quality, clean product that appealed to the populace, but innovation and style diversity suffered.

Lesson 24: Stop by Anchor Brewing, the Tip of the Spear for the US Craft Beer Revolution

In 1871, a recent German immigrant named Gottlieb Brekle purchased a billiard hall in San Francisco and started brewing beer. This brewery transferred ownership numerous times, but it retained the same name: Anchor Brewing. It survived the Great Earthquake of 1906 and the extended hiatus of Prohibition. Yet, it was always on the brink of collapse. That changed in 1965, when Fritz Maytag III, the appliance family's scion, purchased a controlling stake. Maytag poured his personal finances into the company, improving the infrastructure and refocusing on organic ingredients and atypical recipes. In the process, he transformed Anchor into a profitable company and the first American craft brewery. In 2008, he received a James Beard Award for his work at Anchor. If you want to taste a bit of craft history - and their excellent Steam Beer - head over to Potrero Hill in San Francisco for a tour and a brew.

Chapter Review

You can't fully appreciate the modern craft beer scene without some idea of how we got here. Some things to consider as we move forward into the present:

- People have been making beer for almost as long as humans have lived in settled communities. It has been a part of celebrations

and religious ceremonies, and it was vital to making water drinkable.
- In Germany, the parameters of what beer could be were locked in with the sixteenth-century Reinheitsgebot laws, but elsewhere brewing remained a freer, more experimental pursuit.
- Beer was part of America from the beginning, with notable figures as George Washington and Thomas Jefferson brewing in their spare time.
- Prohibition stymied a vibrant, varied beer community and reduced consumer options for decades after repeal.
- You can still drink fine examples of beers from all these historical periods, from Sumerian ales to Colonial recipes to Anchor beer, the first modern craft beer.

And now, we can move on to a primer on beer styles and traditions.

Chapter 3: Understanding Beer Styles and Traditions

One of the major barriers to entry into craft beer is all the terminology. What's the difference between a Stout and a Porter? Why are there, like, ten different types of Pale Ale? What even is a Saison?

So, let's take a moment to look at three major brewing nations and determine what specific styles came from each.

We are also going to look at classic beer examples and their US craft beer equivalents so that you can compare Old World and New at home!

One final note before we begin: I am by no means suggesting that all beer culture originated from a handful of European countries. From Norway to Nigeria, Japan to New Zealand, Jamaica to India, countless cultures and nations have contributed and continue to contribute to the world of beer. It is a quick and dirty guide of traditions and styles that most inform American craft beer.

Still, any discussion of world beer history must begin with this tip:

Lesson 25: Check out Michael Jackson's New World Guide to Beer

There are many fine books about beer. The Ur-text for lovers of all things zymurgical, though, is Michael Jackson's *New World Guide to Beer*. Jackson (clearly the most famous person to bear that name) was a London-based journalist for many years before pivoting to his true passion. He chaired the British Guild of Beer Writers and hosted the television program Beer Hunter. Jackson traveled the world and, through his writing, exploring how culture and beer intersected. His *New World Guide to Beer* is the best cultural investigation of brewing and drinking ever written. I draw extensively from it in this chapter, but you should seek it out yourself. Jackson passed away in 2007.

Lesson 26: Belgium is an Amalgam of Church, Farm, and City Beers.

Perhaps no single nation has a more varied, idiosyncratic beer tradition than Belgium. Like Germany, the US, and the UK, it's an amalgam of different long-independent states with unique cultures and histories. You can see this diversity in their beer. In the northern farmlands of Flanders, you'll find grainy, refreshing Farmhouse Ales. In the more cosmopolitan capital of Brussels, Wild Ales predominate. And dotted throughout the nation are monastery breweries producing rich, decadent abbey ales.

Lesson 27: Compare Two Trappist Abbey Ales, One Belgian and One American

Abbey Ales tend to be malt-forward - often incorporating candi sugar - and redolent of stewed fruit, toffee, and port. We categorize them in terms of their malt bills. Some are blonde, and some are dark. Dubbels have twice the malt pitched in. Tripels have three times the malt. They tend to be lighter-hewed, citric, biscuity, and hot on the tongue. Quadrupels are the strongest and darkest of the bunch. You may have heard of Trappist beer. This designation means that monks brew the ale for the upkeep of their abbey. As of this writing, there are twelve Trappist breweries. Most are Belgian, but there are Italian, Austrian, and Dutch Trappists as well. There's also an American Trappist brewery: Spencer Brewery in Massachusetts. For your, *ahem*, home research, why not grab a Spencer Monk's Reserve Quad and compare it to the top-rated imported Belgian Trappist, Rochefort 10?

Lesson 28: Seek Out the One-Time Best Beer in the World from a Remote Belgian Abbey

If you look up a "Best Beers" list these days, you'll probably see the top spot going to an IPA or Barrel-Aged Stout, which reflects the ascendancy of American craft beer in the broader brewing world. Not so long ago, though, the ale primarily considered to be the "Best Beer in the World" was a Trappist Quad brewed in a remote monastery in West Flanders. The monastery is St. Sixtus, and the beer is

Westvleteren 12. In 2012, I rented a car in Bruges and drove two hours to St. Sixtus. No one is allowed in the monastery, but you can enjoy their beer with a pate sandwich across the street in a cafe called In De Vrede. Westvleteren 12 is a marvel, shockingly light on the tongue for its high ABV and bursting with fruit, coffee, and caramel. Occasionally, the monks of St. Sixtus will ship some "Westy 12" abroad to fund a major building project, but that's exceedingly rare. You might consider buying a bottle of a widely-available Quad brewed from a near-identical recipe, St. Bernardus 12.

Lesson 29: Understanding Lambic-making and Methode Traditionnelle

As mentioned earlier, Belgian Lambic-makers employ an open, wild fermentation technique to produce their sour, funky products. This fermenting process has been refined for generations. It runs in contrast to some of the kettle-souring techniques of many American craft brewers. However, there is a US movement to establish brewing standards based on the process of Belgian Lambic-makers. It is called Methode Traditionnelle. It was created in part to delineate between American ales brewed to the old standards and Belgian outfits that are officially designated at Methode Lambic or Methode Gueuze. Confused? You can think of it like an American vintner making a sparkling wine that meets all the standards of Dom Perignon but not being able to call it Champagne. Anyway, the resulting American Methode outlines everything from fermenting processes to gravities to temperatures. It also forbids artificial flavors and pasteurization.

Lesson 30: Check Out the Work of a Belgian Sour-Maker in Colorado

Want to try an American sour with a genuine Belgian pedigree? You're in luck! In 1996, New Belgium Brewing in Fort Collins, Colorado, tempted over a new master brewer from old Belgium: Peter Bouckaert, who for a decade made beer with Brewery Rodenbach in Roeselare. Bouckaert grew a sour-centric experimental brewing program. One of its best releases was Transatlantique Kriek, a glorious barrel-aged blend of cherry-spiked Lambics from the storied Belgian brewery Oud Beersel. New Belgium released Transatlantique Kriek first in 2003, and they've dropped a new vintage every year since. In 2018, this ale won a gold medal for Best Collaboration beer at the Great American Beer Festival.

Lesson 31: Knowing the Difference Between Saison, Biere de Garde, and Farmhouse Ale

You might have seen these three terms, and they all refer to a relatively high alcohol pale ale originating in the agrarian border region of Belgium and France. Saisons are Belgian, and Bieres de Garde are French. You can reasonably classify both styles a Farmhouse Ales. Traditionally, these beers are brewed with cereal grains in the spring for summer consumption. They are normally under-attenuated, meaning that much of the sugar hasn't converted to ethanol. As such,

Farmhouse Ales have a robust, malty flavor. Sometimes this grain dominates with biscuit and orange-rind notes, while in other cases, the spicy farmhouse yeast takes over. Depending on where the ale ferments, you might find a lot of tartness. These beers originated as fortified ales that farmers would quaff throughout the work months. From the Belgian side of the border, the archetypal example is probably Saison Dupont, while the most prevalent French Farmhouse Ales come from La Choulette.

Lesson 32: Take a Beer Pilgrimage to Hill Farmstead in Vermont

Almost any list of the best American brewers these days includes Hill Farmstead Brewery at or near the top. In Greensboro Bend, Vermont, near the Canadian border, Shaun Hill quietly crafts astonishing Saisons, IPAs, and other ales on his family's farmland. It's hard to find a bad beer from this brewer, but their Farmhouse Ale offerings are fantastic. These ales are vibrant, refreshing, and unique, using on-site well-water, honey, and other local ingredients. I particularly love Anna, a no-nonsense Saison available year-round. It's a semi-arduous journey to reach Hill Farmstead. The final leg is an unpaved road, but you'd be hard-pressed to find a lovelier brewery.

Lesson 33: England Birthed Countless Styles and Exported Them to an Empire

Make your way into a pub during a football match, and you'll see that the English can crush a Light Lager as hard as any Yank, but the grand English beer contribution is in the top-fermenting ale family. England gave us the hoppy Pale Ale, the Porter, and the Russian Imperial Stout. They also pioneered the devilishly easy-drinking Bitter and the heavy-eyelid-inducing Barleywine. English brewers created the gravity-fed Burton Union System, a massive wood-cask fermenting process that still captivates American craft brewers. Probably, no single brewing tradition has influenced the contemporary craft community more than England. Add to this the fact that until the start of the twentieth century, the British Empire extended worldwide. Now you can see how it influenced beer-making from America to India to Honk Kong and beyond.

Lesson 34: CAMRA Keeps the Traditions of the Pub Alive

The Campaign for Real Ale, or CAMRA, advocates for the survival of cask-conditioned ale in pubs; it began in 1971, as the emergence of forced carbonation and kegging threatened to render the cask extinct. Cask-conditioning means that ale goes into the barrel with sugar and yeast still doing their work. Essentially, the beer is alive and developing even as it's being served. Real ale, as it's also known, is hand-pumped and has only natural carbonation. These beers require much care and attention, both in the cellar and on tap. Hence their decline. Their consistency and taste, when served correctly, is transcendent, though, and CAMRA fights to preserve them to this day.

Lesson 35: Make the Journey from Pale Ale to IPA to American IPA

So, you want to know the difference between a Pale Ale and an IPA? Both are made with pale malt and are meant to be consumed fresh. The possibly apocryphal story of the IPA - or India Pale Ale - is that the London brewer George Hodgson chose to give his Pale Ale an extra dose of hops so that it tasted fresher after its long journey from England to India. The IPA was born. This story could be total bunk, but it's what we have!

If you want to taste a classic example of an English Pale Ale, I recommend trying Landlord from Timothy Taylor's Brewery of Yorkshire. It's an earthy, slightly bitter ale. Then, you will want to try a prototypical English IPA. London's Meantime Brewing makes a fine IPA that you can find in most bottle shops. Notice the increase in bitterness and floral notes. Then compare it to a more extravagantly-hopped American example, like Two-Hearted Ale, from Bell's Brewing of Kalamazoo, Michigan. Notice how the late infusion of Centennial hops tempers its bitterness with a pine-needly and grapefruit flavor explosion. That transition from Landlord to Meantime to Two-Hearted is a journey from England to America and traditional to modern.

Lesson 36: What Happened to the Porter?

For a long time, the roasty, black ale know as Porter was almost a family unto itself. English pubs would advertise it separately, as in "Serving Ales and Porter." Throughout the eighteenth and nineteenth centuries, Porter was the signature beer of England. Because of its dark, malt-forward character and higher ABV, Porter was ideal for shipping, and it traveled across the empire. After two World Wars, though, Porter faded both from England and the world at large. Beyond Guinness, you really couldn't find it in most bars. With the rise of craft beer, however, it's made its way back. Not to center-stage exactly, but it's at least out of the wings. If you're in London, consider seeking out Indian Export Porter from The Kernel Brewery, a traditional English Porter with an extra hop kicker. For a modern American example, you need to check out the chocolaty Edmund Fitzgerald Porter from Cleveland's Great Lakes Brewing.

Lesson 37: Stout - What's Imperial in England Versus the US?

First things first: Imperial, in the context of beer, means high-alcohol. The term originated in England in the 1700s, the coinage of brewer Henry Thrale. It was probably a bit of clever marketing. Thrale's outfit produced a robust dark ale that he called Russian Imperial Stout. He claimed it was a favorite of the Russian empress Catherine the Great and that the 10% ABV ensured the stout did not freeze at sea. The term caught on. Today, many IPAs also affix the Imperial moniker when the ABV clicks over 7%. On the American Stout front today, you see a lot of alcohol content that would make Thrale blush. If you want to hit the upper limit of exceptional non-spirit-aged Imperial Stout today, I recommend Dogfish Head's World Wide Stout, a searing, port-like ale that clocks in between 15% and 20%, depending on the year.

Lesson 38: Have a Taste of the Reborn Thomas Hardy's Ale

In the above-mentioned *New World Guide to Beer*, Michael Jackson dedicates a lot of page space to one beer: Thomas Hardy's Ale. Hardy is an Old Ale, a robust dark-malted beer produced intermittently and aged a long time on wood. Families and University Clubs would cellar barrels of Old Ale in anticipation of special occasions or holidays. Such an event occurred in Dorchester in 1968. It was the fortieth anniversary of the writer and favorite son Thomas Hardy's death. Brewer Eldridge Pope commemorated the occasion with an extremely strong Old Ale (many consider it a Barleywine), and at 12.5%, it was one of England's most potent brews. It became a collector's item for beer lovers, a cellar staple. Jackson and countless other writers hosted multi-year vintage vertical tastings. A syrupy, musty potion that burns ever-so-sweetly and mixes plum, toffee, and tobacco notes, Thomas Hardy's Ale is an experience. Unfortunately, it seemed to disappear forever in 2007 when production abruptly halted. Never fear! The ale re-emerged, brewed now by Interbrau of Italy, in 2015. Anyone who's read the deeply depressing Hardy classics *Tess of D'Urbervilles* or *Jude the Obscure* can attest that you need a strong drink after!

Lesson 39: Origin of the Barleywine

The Barleywine ale dates at least to the Victorian Era, and, yes, it is beer. Initially served in smaller bottles called "nips," these extra-strong, wood-aged dark ales were marketed as less expensive alternatives to wine or spirits. They pop with brandy, date, and leather notes. They also have some of the finest names in all of the historic beer: Golden Pride, Old Nick, Bishop's Tipple, and Tally-Ho, to name a few. Stateside today, you can still try some of the original best-sellers. I recommend Yorkshire Stingo, a 9% russet Barleywine brewed by Samuel Smith, from a recipe initially made by Watney. You can compare it to two American Barleywine options. On the one end of the spectrum is Sierra Nevada's outstanding Bigfoot Ale. This massively-hopped ale is abrasively bitter, but it ages like a fine wine. On the other end is the baroque bourbon-barrel Sucaba from Firestone Walker. Velvety and sweet, it takes beer decadence to a new level.

Lesson 40: Take a Bottled Journey Through the English Pub Lineup

I love the English country pub. The cloistered warmth, the middlebrow simplicity, the pride in hospitality - nothing in the world is quite like it. I adore stilling at an enclosed table with friends, enjoying a big meal, and knocking back half-pints of just about everything on draft. When I can't pop off for a vacation in England, I enjoy a pub-handle sampling with these imported gems:

- **Lost Lager (BrewDog)** - The relentlessly self-promoting boys from BrewDog may not be to everyone's taste, but this full-bodied, semi-fruity lager should be.
- **London Pride (Fuller's)** - Ubiquitous for a reason, this Bitter drinks easy and ripples with biting hops.
- **Old Speckled Hen (Greene King)-** Your perfect English Pale. In production since the 1960s, the Hen has a solid amber body and just the right amount of floral hoppiness.
- **Lotus (Ilkley)** - A modern IPA did in the English style. This Yorkshire crew makes lively, esoteric ales with the confidence of old hands.
- **Taddy Porter (Samuel Smith)** - Yes, the Porter still lives! This genuine classic comes in at a belly-warming 5%.
- **Double Stout (Hook Norton)** - A rather delicate Stout, dry and only 5% ABV. This chicory ale pairs admirably with a sticky toffee pudding.
- **Harvest Ale (JW Lees)** - This is your night-ender. A monumental 11.5% Barleywine that is both spicy and sweet, teeming with cherry and nutmeg.

Lesson 41: Seek Out Some Extremely Old German Beers

It can be tempting to dismiss the historic beers of Germany as a convocation of same-ish light lagers. I have fallen victim to this over-simplification myself. The fact is that even within the confines of the Reinheisgebot, German brewers of old produced some flavorful, innovative brews. Even more exciting, many of these centuries-old breweries are still producing and available in stores:

- **Andechser Weissbier Hell (Klosterbrauerei Andechs)** - the Hefeweissen, or wheat lager, is a uniquely German creation. Both slight and heavy, turbid and clean, it bursts with grainy esters. This excellent example comes from a monastic order that began brewing at the dawn of the nineteenth century.
- **Oktoberfest Märzen (Hacker-Schorr)** - Nothing satisfies like a caramel-clear Oktoberfest. There are so many fine examples out there, but I'm partial to this one: one of the official Munich Marzens, produced by a brewery dating the 1400s.
- **Rauchbier Urbock (Aecht Schlenkerla)** - Smoked lagers are truly unique. In this fine example, six-hundred-year-old brewery Schlenkerla smokes caramel malts over beechwood. The result has a little bacon to it and a lot of toffee!
- **Celebrator (Ayinger)** - the Doppelbock is one of the most robustly-malted lagers. It is a near-perfect manifestation: drinkable, delectable, impenetrable. It's from Ayinger, which has operated continuously since the 1800s.
- **Hefeweissbier Dunkel (Weihenstephaner)** - Here's a traditional wheat beer made with darker malts. It has a rich mahogany finish, honey-sweet taste, and fine light body, and it's made by the world's

oldest brewery. Weihenstephaner opened its doors in 1040 as a monastery operation and hasn't looked back since.

Lesson 42: The Eisbock Creates a High-ABV Brew with the Power of Ice!

When discussing Belgian and English beer, we hit upon several styles that register high alcohol content. Many involve long-term barrel aging, inflated malt bills, and sugar-heavy adjuncts. Well, Germany has its answer to these strong ales, and it is the Eisbock. The Eisbock is a dark brew, similar to the Doppelbock, that undergoes a distillation process. But unlike whiskey, which is distilled by boiling off water from the mash, an Eisbock is concentrated through freezing. Water freezes at a higher temperature than ethanol, so when brewers chill the Bock, the unfrozen liquid has a higher ABV. The Eisbock is often fruity and spicy, but it is always syrupy and burns on the way down. Tap 9 Aventinus Eisbock is a widely-distributed, well-rated, 12% ABV offering from Schneider Weisse.

Lesson 43: Consider the Difference Between a Traditional Pilsner, a Macro-Market Pilsner, and a Craft Pilsner

In the last chapter, we explored how the German-inspired lagers came to dominate the American beer scene in the twentieth century. However, it is a colossal mistake to liken all light lagers to that accursed Bud Light. So, let's try one more comparison. Find someplace with a decent selection of imported beer, and purchase a bottle of Ayinger's excellent Bavarian Pils. It is a perfect example of the German Pilsner style, from a recipe that's been honed and refined for decades. Now compare that to a macro-market American Pilsner, Miller Genuine Draft. I'm actually a fan of good ol' MGD, but there's no comparing. You cannot ignore the prevalence of adjuncts like rice and corn syrup after enjoying a Pils made with real Pilsner malts. For good measure, I also recommend you grab a modern craft Pilsner to compare. My personal standby is Post Shift Pilsner from Jack's Abby Craft Lagers in Framingham, Massachusetts.

Chapter Review

That was a lot of information, I know. Trust me, though: a good background in international brewing traditions will serve you well as you dig into American craft beer. Still, don't feel like you have to be a beer historian to step into a taproom. Here are some simple takeaways:

- Belgium's beer traditions are as varied as the disparate states that comprise it. From Saisons to Sours to Trappist Ales, you will find them flavorful and strong.
- Probably the most complex and intricately-made Belgian ale is the Lambic. American brewers approximate the spontaneous fermentation techniques of the Belgians with the Methode Traditionnelle.
- England's brewers crafted and exported such influential styles at the Pale Ale, IPA, Imperial Stout, Porter, Bitter, and Barleywine.
- The Campaign for Real Ale (CAMRA) has fought for years to preserve the pub tradition of cask-conditioned ale in the UK.
- Even accounting for the repressive Reinheisgebot laws, German beer has varied, flavorful, innovative styles like the Marzen, Rauchbier, Hefeweizen, Doppelbock and Eisbock.

Okay, take a breath. We're entering the era of American Craft beer.

Chapter 4: The Modern American Craft Beer Movement

We've taken a trip from Mesopotamia to the unification of Germany, from the British Empire to the newly liberated United States. We've made it to the Twenty-First Amendment, repealing Prohibition.

Now, it's time to dig into the modern American craft beer movement.

Lesson 44: Brewing in Secret, even after Repeal

On December 5, 1933, Prohibition ended. Brewers began legally operating again. Yet, homebrewing remained a legal gray area in much of America. In 1978, making beer at home was finally exempted from federal taxation. (Thank you, Jimmy Carter!) State-to-state, homebrewers faced legal ramifications for years afterward, though. The last states to legalize it fully were Alabama and Mississippi, both in 2013. During these dicier years, amateur beermakers relied on under-the-radar tips and tactics. Tim Matson and Lee Ann Dorr chronicle this period in the excellent *Mountain Brew: A High-Spirited Guide to Country-Style Beer Making*. Detailing practices from mid-century Vermont, the book talks about growing hops at home and a not-so-subtle Blue Ribbon malt product that contained hops.

Lesson 45: Get a Homebrew Kit!

We talk a lot about personal liberty in the country. It's such a central tenet of the American experience that it has taken on a lot of ambiguous, even insidious interpretations. Nonetheless, if you're reading this book, it's probably safe to assume that you view the liberty to brew your beer as a good thing. So, take advantage of it!

If you want to brew beer today, you can do so fairly simply. You don't need glass carboys and huge kettles for steeping grain. All you need are a couple of plastic fermenting buckets, a hydrometer, some plastic tubes, and a bottle capper. Outfits like Northern Brewer will sell you that for less than a hundred bucks. You can purchase a partial mash recipe kit - including yeast, hop pellets, a little malted grain, and some malt extract - for under fifty dollars. With that small investment, you can make a couple of gallons of ale in your garage or your apartment's kitchen. It's a small investment for a lot of fun and some beer you crafted yourself. After a couple of batches, you may want to try a full-grain brew. Soon after that, you might be developing your recipes and printing labels. The sky is the limit!

Lesson 46: Try Two Watershed Brews from the First Contemporary Craft Brewers

As noted in Chapter 2, the first modern craft brewery was established with Anchor Brewing's transformation in the 1960s and 70s. Yet, the 1980s saw the emergence of two beer giants that forever changed how Americans drink. You have probably enjoyed both of their flagship beers before, but I recommend reacquainting yourself with them. They're even better than you remember.

Sierra Nevada Pale Ale

Following decades of lagers, this beer was a lightning flash. Ken Grossman and partner Paul Camusi started brewing commercially in Chico, California, in 1979, working off a jerry-rigged system. Their flagship Pale Ale was bitter in a way that shocked the popular palate. Packed with West Coast Cascade hops, you'll detect a balanced forest and fruit quality. It's incredible to have something so robust be so drinkable.

Samuel Adams Boston Lager

On the other side of the country in 1984, Jim Koch and Rhonda Kallman founded Boston Beer Company and rolled out a revelatory lager. Just as the Sierra Nevada had shocked drinkers with a style that has been sorely lacking for decades, Boston Beer recalibrated what Americans conceived a lager to be. They incorporated darker malts for a more caramel-forward liquid and hopped it with floral, spicy German hops. Boston Lager is both smooth and aggressive, refreshing and energizing.

Lesson 47: How the Number of American Breweries Exploded this Century

When the Sierra Nevada and the Boston Beer Company were opening shop, there were barely one hundred operating breweries in the United States. Boy, has that changed! From the eighties to today, seven thousand breweries opened across the country, double the number of operators before Prohibition. Between 2006 and 2016, employment in the beer industry grew by 70%. And while Americans drink less beer today than they did a decade ago, craft beer has a larger share of this consumption. Why the massive proliferation? In part, we have seen the repeal and reform of laws that restricted beer production, distribution, and sales. You can thank the brewers themselves and their industry group, the Brewers Association, for lobbying elected officials to change these regulations. There's also a strong demand component. Forerunner brewers piqued American interest in flavorful, potent beer, giving quality micro-brewers a market to sell to, which drove more demand. That self-propelling cycle has continued for many decades now.

Lesson 48: What is the Three-Tier System?

When we think of selling beer, we imagine that a brewer makes the beverage, then the consumer buys it at a store. Unfortunately, in the US, it's not that simple. Before Prohibition, many saloons were brewery-run. Your local watering hole might have been a Stroh's spot, and that was the beer you drank there. After Prohibition Repeal, the government sought ways to prevent the return of the old brewer-owned bar and to enable tighter regulation and taxation for alcohol. So, they implemented a Three-Tier System: producers make beer, distributors transport it, and retailers sell it. Each tier must be separately-owned and operated.

This complicated system has opened the door to plenty of gaming and manipulation. As mentioned earlier, large conglomerates like AB-InBev have their own distribution network. It's legally separate from the brewing operations, but it essentially exists to deliver the products of Budweiser and their acquired brands. It is an extremely powerful operation, and it's chillingly effective at monopolizing shelves and tap-lines. The Three-Tier System has also stymied small brewery operations and marketing.

A craft brewer can't pour you a beer or sell you a six-pack on-site in many states. Luckily, some small operations have worked out relief with their home states. In New York, for example, small brewers are allowed to self-distribute to bars and restaurants. And since the market disruption of COVID-19, many breweries nationwide can now ship directly to consumers.

Lesson 49: The most popular styles in America today

We're not living in the same beer world we did in the late twentieth century. We no longer have to settle for the same adjunct lager style on the shelves. So, what are the most popular beer styles in America now? According to Untappd, the popular beer rating application, the most check-in beers are:

- **#1-#5 are all some form of hoppy Pale Ale or IPA**. The rise in IPA popularity and the speed at which it is developing is the dominant narrative of American craft beer.
- **#6 - Fruited Sour**. It could be the previously discussed Methode Traditionnelle Lambic styles or a faster-fermenting "kettle sour."
- **#7 - Imperial Stout**. High-gravity, adjunct-heavy, barrel-aged - Stouts have been on the rise for twenty years. Today they are bigger and crazier than ever.
- **#8 - Session IPA**. With the meteoric rise of Founder's All Day IPA in the early 2010s, America discovered it wanted a hoppy ale that was as light as a Bud.
- **#9 - Belgian Tripel**. It is an outlier. Tripels are neither hoppy nor are they generally amended with wild ingredients or spirit aging. It's cool that they cracked the Top 10!
- **#10 - European Pale Lager**. Another pleasant surprise. These lagers are normally slightly stronger and more aggressively hopped than their Bavarian brethren.

Lesson 50: Diversity in American Craft Beer

Here's a sobering stat, courtesy of the Brewers Association: 84% of American craft brewery staff is white. Moreover, 88% of all craft brewery owners are white, as are 89% of all Head Brewers.

Indeed, this lack of representation is terrible in and of itself. The practical concern is that good beer should appeal to all backgrounds and demographics, yet that simply hasn't materialized. You will find plenty of beers named after Tupac and Jay-Z lyrics, but there's a good chance the beer was developed, brewed, and served by a white person. And there's nearly as good of a chance that the person ordering the craft beer is also white.

Kevin Blodger, co-owner, and director of brewing operations at Union Craft Brewing in Baltimore and former chair of the BA's Diversity Committee (he's still a member) theorizes that this lack of representation is organic. Craft beer spreads by word-of-mouth, and people tend to interact with those that look like them, live in their neighborhoods, and – perhaps most importantly – exist in the same socioeconomic class. Starting a craft brewery requires independent wealth or ready access to business credit, so most of the public faces have been affluent white folks. They start breweries in affluent neighborhoods and hire folks similar to themselves.

The Brewers Association is working to counter the imbalance by funding diversity fellowships and mentor programs. And beer-workers of color are networking, speaking out, and establishing an out-front presence in the community. However, this lack of diversity is as pernicious in beer as in virtually all industrial and social venues. Beer drinkers owe it to themselves to engage with the ongoing conversation. If you want to get a sense of the challenges and priorities of minority workers in craft beer, I recommend following the folks at *Beer Kulture* on social media (https://www.beerkulture.com/). This group funds and fosters workshops, scholarships, and discourse about the role people of color play in the community.

Lesson 51: Seek Out Special Brews from the Pink Boots Society

In 2007, Teri Fahrendorf quit her job as the head brewer at Steelhead Brewing in Eugene, Oregon, and took to the road. She visited over seventy breweries nationwide as a guest brewer, and more often than not, she found herself paired with another woman, usually the only woman at the brewhouse. Throughout her travels, Teri wore a pair of pink boots that her mother gifted her. At the end of this road-brewing journey, she had a list of women passionate about beer but often isolated and marginalized within their organizations. She founded the Pink Boots Society. PBS began as a networking organization for women in beer, a venue to share best practices and experiences.

Since then, it has developed into a non-profit that funds and distributes scholarships for female beer-workers. Its leadership is composed of industry professionals volunteering their time. PBS hosts workshops and meetings and – perhaps unfortunately – serves as a public face responding to too-frequent instances of hostility, inequality, and misogyny in brewing.

On March 8th, International Women's Day, the Society partners with supporting breweries and Yakima Hops for a worldwide Pink Boots Collaboration Brew. Local chapters "put on their pink boots, and brew their chosen beer style." Proceeds from beer sales go to fund programming and scholarships. To support this great organization – by drinking a tasty beer! – find your local participating brewery at https://www.pinkbootssociety.org/pink-boots-brew/.

One final note: today, only about 14% of US craft brewery management and production staff identify as female, according to the Brewers Association.

Lesson 52: IPAs - Taste the East Coast vs. West Coast Rivalry

The IPA is such a prevalent style that, in a relatively short span of time, it has spawned countless sub-styles: Session IPAs, Hazy IPAs, Brut IPAs, Black IPAs. The major twenty-first-century story of the IPA is the East Coast versus West Coast split. As craft beer gained popularity in the US, the West Coast - and California, in particular - became home turf for hopped-up IPAs. A standard style began to develop, with lots of early-boil hops and a robust malt base to temper the taste-bud-searing bitterness. Because of this, American IPAs tended to be stronger. Brewers added clarifying agents to give them a glassy, clean appearance; this was the West Coast IPA. It was boozy, intensely bitter and fruity, amber in hue and clear. Some prototypical examples are:

- **Ballast Point Brewing's Sculpin IPA** - a 7% grapefruit-forward crusher. Perfect with a greasy meal.
- **Stone Brewing's Ruination Double IPA** - an iron-fisted piney-bitter 8.5% brew. Drink it slowly.
- **Russian River Brewing's Pliny the Elder** - one of the most elegant, balanced IPAs ever made. It's 8%, but it drinks like it's 4%, with a delicate body, assertive bittering, and hop notes of both citrus and flower.

Flash forward to the early 2010s, and a new type of Pale emerges in and around New England. It's normally unfiltered, giving it a hazy, juice-like appearance. The hop balance is different, with more immersions later in the boil and during fermentation. The result is much less bitter. So, the East Coast, or New England, IPA is born. When you hear about a Hazy IPA, this is it. Turbid, fluffy, and super flavorful - here are some of the best examples:

- **Lawson's Finest Liquids' Sip of Sunshine** - The juiciest of the juicy IPAs, bursting with orange and clocking in at 8%.
- **Other Half Brewing's Mylar Bags** - At 8.8%, it's as muscular as the NEIPA gets. It is spiked with wheat and bursting with passion-fruit and lemongrass.
- **Sierra Nevada's Hazy Little Thing IPA** - The West Coast can do a mean East Coaster, it seems, with a moderate 6.5% radiant gold ale popping with pine-forward hop flavor.

Lesson 53: Who Still Makes an Unflavored Stout?

The last decade has seen the rise of the embellished stout. Search your local bottle shop, and you will find Breakfast Stouts, Mexican Stouts, Pastry Stouts, and so many Barrel-Aged Stouts. There's nothing wrong with these varieties. I'll be spotlighting many of them in the coming chapters. But the question remains, where can you find a high-quality, unflavored Stout? They still exist, and here are a few that you need to check out ASAP:

- **Left Hand Brewing's Milk Stout**- Looking for the smoothness of a Guinness with a bit more punch? Check out this silken 6% milk stout. For added vivacity, pick up some nitro-infused cans.
- **Bell's Brewing's Expedition Stout** - Fresh off the assembly line, this 10.5% Imperial Stout kicks with coffee and blackberry undertones. But it develops brilliantly in the cellar, mellowing and taking on brownie and caramel qualities.
- **North Coast Brewing's Old Rasputin** - There's a powerful wallop of dark chocolate and umami in this oily black Russian Imperial Stout, and you feel every bit of its 9% ABV.
- **Great Divide Brewing's Yeti Imperial Stout** - Can a huge 9.5% Ale still feel light and nuanced? Yeti sure can, with a melange of cocoa, hazelnut, wheat, and just a bit of hop bitterness.

Lesson 54: Experience Sour Ales Made Without Open Fermentation

We've discussed at length the traditional coolship, open-fermented Lambics, but don't assume that an excellent sour beer must be produced using the Methode Traditionnelle. Craft brewers use many fermentation techniques to create exceptional sour ales. The Rare Barrel uses mixed fermentation, aging ales in wooden barrels with wild cultures like Brettaonomyces or lactobacillus. Others choose a quicker route, pitching these wild cultures into the fermenting vessel. The term "kettle sour" can seem like a pejorative, dismissing brewers that elect a faster souring process. Some styles lend themselves to the practice, especially light Germanic sours like the Gose and the Berliner Weisse. J. Wakefield Brewing in Miami has a line of kettle-soured Berliners that have won multiple awards.

Lesson 55: Check out Some Near-Defunct Styles That Are Coming Back!

In the last couple of chapters, I've mentioned styles like the Saison, Gose, and Berliner Weisse. These are traditional styles that were all but extinct a few decades ago. American craft brewers played a significant role in reviving them. Here's a rundown of some excellent American revivals:

Berliner Weisse

Grimm Artisan Ales has a series of vanilla-infused Berliners called Pop! Sweet and sour in equal measure, Blackberry Pop! is a particularly delightful entry.

Gose

A wheat ale fermented with coriander and a little salt, this style may sound odd. But try Westbrook Brewing's excellent, straightforward Gose, and you'll see the light.

Grisette

This French farmhouse ale – similar to the Biere de Garde – was popular among factory workers. Saint Adairius's slightly tart Girl in Grey pays tribute to that history.

Grodziskie

A smoky pale Polish wheat beer, this style is having a mini-rival lately. New Belgium and Three Floyds Brewing recently collaborated on one, called Grätzer Ale (an alternate style name).

Gruit

Dating to the Middle Ages, this style is heavy on berries and replaces hops with plants and spices. Portland, Oregon's Upright Brewing makes Special Herbs, a Gruit with orange peel, lemongrass, hyssop, and peppercorns, aged in gin barrels.

Saison

Probably no near-defunct style has revived as completely as the Saison. A widely-available, delightful producer of Saisons is Denver's Crooked Stave Artisanal Ales. Their sour oak-aged ale Surette is unparalleled.

Chapter Review

In many ways, the modern craft beer movement is a contradiction. It challenged and largely unseated the hegemonic dominance of macro-brewers, but its ethos of innovative, interesting brewing faces the challenge of few dominant styles flooding the market:

- Along with Anchor Brewing, the Sierra Nevada and the Boston Beer company blew up the beer world, redefining the Pale Ale and the Lager, respectively.
- Even after Prohibition, would-be brewers faced considerable systemic challenges, from regulations effectively outlawing homebrewing to a Three-Tier System for sales and distribution.
- The IPA grew popular incredibly quickly and morphed into many sub-styles, including an East Coast vs. West Coast divide.
- The Imperial Stout continues to proliferate and develop. While many today are spirit-aged or loaded with adjuncts, you can still find many fantastic straight Stouts.

- The Sour Ale, which is a crazily broad group to consider, is also super popular. These ales involve many different traditions, methods, and ingredients.
- A huge benefit of the American craft beer movement is the revival of nearly-extinct styles, including the Saison, Gose, and Gruit.

It looks like we're caught up to the present day. How about we take a trip to a contemporary craft beer taproom?

Chapter 5: How to Approach a Taproom

Here we go. You're now confident that you can tell an IPA from a Porter, a Fruited Sour from a Biere de Garde. You know what goes into beer and what makes it crisp or bitter or roasty.

Hopefully, you are now excited and thirsty, ready to belly up to the counter of your local taproom!

Here's a polite reminder that, despite all the historical and style information I have given you in the last few pages, this should not feel like homework. It's all meant to demystify the terms and descriptors you might find in the brewery. So, please: have fun! Bring some friends along and have a designated driver or rideshare lined up for afterward.

Lesson 56: Make Your First Visit When the Place is Less Busy

The taproom you're visiting wants you to feel at home. Even with well-rated, hip, and popular breweries, the staff genuinely wants to attend to your needs. If you're a newbie, they will help you navigate their tap list. However, no matter how conscientious or friendly the workforce, it will be strained if they are filled to capacity. You probably won't find the service and assistance you want if you show up in the early afternoon on a beautiful Saturday. To guarantee yourself the nicest inaugural experience possible, try to visit when it's not mobbed. Avoid rush mealtimes. Show up at the opening. Try to do a weekday, if you can manage it. Also, if you arrive and the taproom is crazy, see if they do brewery tours. It is a great way to familiarize yourself with the brewer and kill some time while the crowd thins a bit.

Lesson 57: Know Whether You're Visiting a Generalist or Specialist Brewer

Here's a personal story. I celebrated my bachelor party with some buddies in Stowe, Vermont. In addition to being an absolutely beautiful region, this area produces some of the best Pale Ales globally. Hop-heads from all over the country travel there year-round to sample the brews. As my friends and I crossed into Vermont from New Hampshire, we stopped in Brattleboro. There, we stopped at a relatively new establishment called Hermit Thrush Brewery. They had only been open a year, and their portfolio focused exclusively on Belgian-style ales. There was not a Pale in the house. We settled in for a round of Sours, Abbey Ales, and Saisons. It was great, but as we hung at the bar, numerous folks came in asking what IPAs they had on tap. Most left annoyed that the hop-bombs they heard so much about were not available. If only they had entered with either open minds or a little advanced research, they might have stuck around for some fantastic brews.

Twenty years ago, you could walk into a craft brewery taproom and expect a pretty diverse selection. You'd generally find a Pale Ale, a Porter or Stout, probably an Amber Ale, etc. Today, however, many brewers focus on one or two styles. Trillium Brewing in Boston is almost entirely about Stouts and East Coast IPAs.

Except for a few high-profile Pales, Russian River's portfolio is nearly all sour. You can even find some magnificent brewers that stick to lagers, like Von Trappe Brewing, Bierstadt Lagerhaus, and Jack's Abby. So, before you set foot in the door, know if you're entering a generalist brewer with many different styles or a specialist with only one or two.

Lesson 58: Find Out What the Stable Beers Are

Innovation and experimentation are endemic to almost all craft breweries. A particular outfit might put out scores of awesome one-off beers each year. Regardless of how prolific the brewer is, however, they still have a stable of regular offerings. It's important to find out what the stable options are, either in advance or from the staff. For example, Against the Grain Brewery has a well-earned reputation for producing lots of weird, innovative beers. If you're hitting up their taproom, you probably should start with their popular standbys like Citra Ass Down! IPA and 35K Milk Stout. These will give you a sense of their house style and get you ready for the wackier offerings.

Lesson 59: Let the Taproom Worker be Your Guide

Taproom workers know more about beer than almost anyone. As a rule, craft breweries pride themselves on training every staff member to understand and discuss the product. Tell them what you like, what you're curious about, and what you've heard about the brewery. They will be able to guide you through the taps. Probably, they can offer some more general wisdom. Many breweries foot the bill for advanced beer server training like the Cicerone Program. You might have the ale equivalent of a sommelier in training pouring your pint.

Lesson 60: Sample Before You Select

When you're new to an establishment, it can be uncomfortable to ask for a sample. At a craft beer taproom, you should overcome that discomfort. High-quality beer isn't cheap, and many brewers don't distribute it. So, you're likely going to be choosing from a list of unknown, pricey options. Even if you're getting a suggestion from the beer-tender, feel free to ask to try a sample pour. Trust me. That server would much rather give you an ounce or two of beer than serve you a full pour of something you don't want. Just be sure to tip generously!

Lesson 61: Save Your Palate by Drinking in the Right Order

I mentioned Other Half Brewing in an earlier chapter. They are much-praised brewer in Red Hook, Brooklyn. Their original warehouse space can be seen in Goodfellas' late scene (decades before they occupied it). I lived a few blocks from this space when they opened shop in 2014. One weeknight, I sauntered over to grab some growlers. I asked the woman behind the counter if I could sample some ales, and she said sure. Immediately, I asked to try their most-hyped IPA at the time, All Green Everything. She halted me, pouring their house IPA first. She wanted to take me through their main lineup and warned that the 10% Triple IPA I'd just asked for would kill my tastebuds for anything I tried later. Boy, was she looking out for me!

One moral of this story is, of course, to trust your beer-tender. The second lesson is to consider your palate as you drink. Don't start with something insanely bitter, sour, boozy, or cloyingly sweet. Think in terms of the handful of things you intend to try throughout the visit, then go from most delicate to most intense. For good measure, check with your server what drinking order they'd recommend.

Lesson 62: Pay Attention to the Glassware

Remember when everything just came in a chunky shaker pint with a faded Budweiser frog on it? Those days are long gone, and one of the tremendous educational opportunities of a taproom visit is seeing the glassware the brewery chooses to serve its beverages in. Many will put everything in a twelve-ounce snifter, a glass shape that's both resilient and ideal for retaining the beer's bouquet. Others may have English-style pints for their Pales or Tulips for their Sours. Your more modern IPA-heavy operations may have pricier Teku or Spiegelau glasses. The aforementioned Bierstadt Lagerhaus in Denver went so far as to commission specially-designed glasses for each of their three stable lagers. They insist that not only their taproom workers but also the bars they distribute use them.

Lesson 63: Know When to Call It a Day

I would be hard-pressed to think of a more fun way to spend an afternoon than quaffing half the tap list of a new brewery. We are living through an exciting time for beer-drinkers. Each new brewery that opens is potentially world-class, and more are opening daily. So, while I would hate to throw cold water on any taproom session, it is essential to know your limits. That first beer will be amazing, and probably the second will be even better. However, once you get to four or five brews in, you might be swaying on your feet. An excellent start to tempering this is to drink slow, hydrate between beers, and eat!

But it would help if you also had the personal discretion to throw in the towel when it's time. No one wants to be the person who keels over at the bar. Nor will it improve anyone's taproom experience if the staff asks them to leave. Also, remember: craft beer writ large is stronger than Coors. You can't crush it all day. Be responsible. Know when to call it a day. Don't drive home after a day at the beer bar.

Lesson 64: Grab Something for Home

Not to speak too optimistically, but you're pretty certain to find at least one beer you love at any given taproom. Hopefully, you will find several! So, don't forget to grab something on the way out the door. Here are your most likely to-go options:

Cans and Bottles

Nothing too crazy here! In particular, sixteen-ounce cans are popular among craft brewers. They are ideal for storing hoppy beers. Bottles are more common these days with dark ales and beers containing live yeast, like Sours. Three notes of caution, though:

1. Check with the staff when beers were packaged to make sure you get the freshest product.
2. Be wary of palettes of packaged beer sitting out un-refrigerated. Unless they were just pulled from a walk-in fridge, they might be faded.
3. Many hip brewers lately are experimenting with packaged beer smoothies, with fruit puree added to beer before canning.

Fruit contains sugar, which will react to live yeast and produce carbon dioxide. It builds up, increasing pressure in cans. See where I'm headed? There have been reports - too many, in fact - of these cans exploding.

Growlers

As old as the country itself, these glass containers are a great way to carry away some draft beer for home. Most establishments will fill any clean growler you bring. Some insist on using their own. It could be a matter of quality control, not wanting to risk their beer deteriorating because of light or oxygen infiltration. The best growler systems, in my opinion, are Counter Pressure. They spread beer around the edge of the growler interior, preventing foaming, and they remove much of the air left behind after filling.

These systems require a particular size of screw-top growler, though. Breweries using them may require you to purchase one. Unlike capped bottles, growlers don't retain carbonation indefinitely. You'll want to finish them within a few days.

Crowlers

It's an oversized aluminum can, filled and sealed on-site from the tap. The pros of this option are many. It's durable, tightly-sealed, and keeps light fully out. While a crowler is not reusable like a glass growler, it is nonetheless recyclable. The one con of a crowler is that, once you've cracked it, you need to finish the job. So, plan accordingly!

Lesson 65: Update Your Wardrobe While You're There

Call me a nerd. Call me un-stylish. Call me a shill to craft beer (all three statements are probably accurate), but I think that most brewery apparel rocks. Think of it this way. Craft brewers need their products to stand out, and most of them value local partners. So you see a lot of hand-drawn graphic design, much of it seriously beautiful. I love the candy-colored designs of Half Acre Brewing and the nineties graffiti art of LIC Beer Project. Get yourself a shirt, hat, or hoodie with that artwork on it. Do it!

Chapter Review

Once again, a craft beer taproom can be a little intimidating if you're unfamiliar with the product. With a little preparation and an open mind, it can provide a truly awesome experience. Some things to remember:

- Try to avoid the busiest taproom times for your first visit. It will put you and your server in a position to have the best possible experience.
- Do a little research on the brewery beforehand, so you know what kind of beer they do and do not make.
- Take your server's advice about the offerings and the order you drink them in. And don't be afraid to sample before you purchase.
- Know your limit. Leave when you've reached that limit, and travel safely.
- Don't forget to grab a growler, a four-pack, and a branded shirt on your way out the door.

Chapter 6: Knowing Your Metrics

You've had the opportunity to visit a few breweries, peruse a good bottle shop, and hunkered down at a high-end beer bar. At this point, you probably have a much better sense of what you like and don't like in craft beer.

You might prefer a beer that quenches your thirst or one that warms you up. You might want one that's bright and fruity or one that's rich and complex. You may relish pairing a brew with your lunch or cracking one at the end of the night over a book.

There's no wrong way to enjoy beer, as long as you're doing it responsibly.

Now, the combination of historical knowledge and personal preference can open you to a world of exploration. Let's dive a little deeper into the metrics and components that make a particular beer taste look, smell, taste, and feel the way it does.

Lesson 66: Tour Some Breweries

The surest way to glean a lot of beer-brewing information is to visit some breweries. We already discussed the experience of hitting up a craft beer taproom. But what about the brewery itself? You can learn so much about the composition and evolving practices of beer-making from walking a brewing floor. Not every tour is the same, though. Some brewers don't give tours at all, and others just give you a walk-through of the floor with a talk about the company's history. There's nothing wrong with that; it can be quite interesting. Still, I prefer something with more detail about the process.

Here's my favorite brewery tour experience ever. In 2013, a buddy of mine was getting married, and we decided to spend a long weekend rafting and camping in Nova Scotia. On the final day, we took an early-morning ferry across the Bay of Fundy, which landed at St. John, New Brunswick. It was midmorning, and we were both hungry and a bit hungover. We happened upon a gastropub with a small brewery attached. It was called Big Tide Brewing, and brewer Wendy Papadopoulos was transferring the wort for a seasonal Pumpkin Ale into a fermentation tank.

Wendy saw that we were checking out the brewing system and invited us for an impromptu tour of the two-room setup. In the process, she went through the malt bill for the Pumpkin Ale. We sniffed to bags of malted grain and chewed on the waterlogged spent grain. She gave each of us a taster of the unfermented wort. Then, over Reuben sandwiches, my buddy and I drink two pints of the finished beer. Pumpkin Ales are not my favorite beers, but having sampled each component of this well-crafted ale in advance, I could enjoy this one with a deeper appreciation.

One final note: you might also derive some seriously useful knowledge by touring distilleries. In particular, whiskey-making involves similar practices and ingredients to beer-making.

Lesson 67: What Water is Best for Beer?

When considering the ingredients that go into beer, it is both easy and insane to forget water. After all, beer is water steeped with grain and hops, then left to ferment with yeast. So, choosing what water to brew with must be pretty important, right? The adage warns us: "garbage in, garbage out," which pretty much sums up the stakes for water in beer. It affects mouthfeel and taste, durability, and longevity. The water needs to be around 5 pH, the ideal range for converting malt enzymes into sugar. Also, darker beers have more acidic malts, so the water needs a higher pH. Hoppy beers require a slightly lower pH to prevent astringency. Harder, more mineral-heavy water produces a beer with better stability, but these minerals affect pH. It's a balancing act. Professional brewers spend a lot of time filtering and augmenting their water to get their wort started right.

Lesson 68: Regions with Great Beer Water!

Some parts of the world just plain-straight have great water for brewing. You shouldn't be surprised, then, that the regions you associate with good beer also have killer H2O. For example, Pilsen's water is low-pH and low-sulfate. It's perfect for the light, grainy Pilsner. Burton-on-Trent, famous for its wood-aged Pale Ales, has water with a higher sulfate count that's great for hoppy beers. Dublin's water has an incredibly low pH, so brewers in the Irish capital needed to balance it out with lots of dark malts. Can you think of a pitch-black Ale from Dublin that's pretty popular?

In Belgium, one of the coolest water facts involves St. Bernardus Abbey Ales. You may recall from Chapter 3 that St. Bernardus makes a Belgian Quad using an identical recipe to the storied Westvleteren 12. Well, this Watou brewer has a crazy water source, too. They pull it from a 500-foot-deep on-site artesian well. Scientists have noted that this well contains water that originated from rainfall during the time of Joan of Arc!

Lesson 69: Check Out Ingredients at a Homebrew Store

There aren't quite as many stores for homebrewers these days. Ten years ago, a Whole Foods near my work carried malted grain and hops that you could buy with a scoop, like coffee! Now you might need to travel a couple of towns over to find a decent brewer's supply store. Even if you don't brew beer yourself, I recommend poking your head into one of these establishments. For someone working to understand why they like certain types of beers, the opportunity to see, smell and handle beer ingredients is invaluable. Running your hands through Two-Row Malt or Flaked Barley will change the way you view a beer. Like East Coast IPAs? Try shoving your sniffer into a punch of Mosaic hops.

Much like taproom staff, brewing supply workers are almost always psyched to assist new customers. Be careful, though: you might go in there for a little research and reconnaissance and walk out with supplies for your first home batch!

Lesson 70: A Malt of Every Style

You can't have beer without the four main components: water, malted grain, hops, and yeast. All four are essential. However, when we think about a beer style's distinguishing features - its color, ABV, thickness, aroma, and taste - the malt is operative across the board. Let's look at some popular craft beer styles and discuss how specific malts are key in making them:

Pale Ales and IPAS

Unsurprisingly, you would use a lighter grain for a Pale Ale. The most common malt choices in America are the ever-popular 2-Row Brewers Malt. It's light in hue, efficient in wort production, and mellow in flavor. Two-Row produces an adjustable cereal base for hops to play against, while Pale Ale Malt produces a slightly darker wort. More delicate IPAs sometimes incorporate the even lighter Pilsner Malt.

Stout

Even in the demonstrably darker Stout, 2-Row makes an appearance, but it's generally in concert with Roasted Barley, Black Malt, and Chocolate Malt. These darker malts impart a roasty, rich, full-bodied character. You might also find some Crystal, Maris-Otter, and Caramel Malts. You see, since the Stout is such a malt-forward style, the bill is more about creating a complex grain profile than providing a simple platform for other components.

Farmhouse Ale

As you might remember, Farmhouse Ales were traditionally made at the start of the growing season for consumption in the field. It shouldn't be a surprise, then, that the malt bill for these beers generally involves many different grains. Of course, you can expect to find our old friend 2-Row, but you'll also see Vienna Malt, Wheat and Oats. Malted Rye is common as well. Look at these ingredients, and consider how they taste in food. Think of wheat, rye, or multigrain bread. A sweet, spicy, fulsome character emerges from this malt mixture.

Lesson 71: Measuring Gravity in Beer

Determining the alcohol content of a beer is all about measuring gravity. By this, I mean you find out how dense the wort is after the boil, then you see how this density goes down over time. As the yeast eats the sugar from the malt-bill, the liquid's gravity decreases.

If you've ever brewed at home, you know how to use a hydrometer. This instrument looks like a thermometer, but it has a weighted bulb at the bottom. The higher the hydrometer sits in a wort sample, the denser the wort is, and the more sugar is yet to burn. Brewers measure in terms of Original Gravity (the density after brewing) and Final Gravity (the density once fermentation is complete). The difference between these two gravities reveals the Alcohol by Volume for the finished beer.

Lesson 72: History of the Hop

In many ways, the hop plant is a truly unique beer ingredient. Whiskey uses malt, similar to beer. Yeast goes into pretty much any alcoholic beverage, while water goes into pretty much every beverage, period. Hops, however, are the definitive beer staple. They impart bitterness and particular flavor notes. These flavors can be spicy, resinous, fruity, candied, earthy, floral, herbal, or any combination. There are currently about eighty different hop varieties, each with its signature flavor profile.

When did humanity first become aware of the hop?

Famously, the Roman naturalist Pliny the Elder mentions the hop plant's existence as a wild-growing weed. The first known use of hops in brewing is in 736 in Germany. Soon farmers were cultivating the plant for beer production across Europe. England, however, banned the domestic growth of hops until the sixteenth century. Today, farmers cultivate hop plants at an industrial scale in Continental Europe, the British Isles, Australia, New Zealand, the US, and beyond.

Modern brewers often eschew whole-cone hops in favor of compressed pellets, lupulin tinctures, oils, or powders. I'll cover these technological advances later!

Lesson 73: What is Dry-Hopping?

Set foot in just about any craft brewery, and you are likely to hear the term dry-hopping. So, what is that? Remember back to those early IPAs being shipped from England to India? Often, whole hop cones were dropped into the Pale Ale cask before ships pulled up anchor. Soaking in the fermenting ale, these hop plants imparted lots of green, raw lupulin flavors. What they didn't impart was bitterness. After all, bittering hops must be added early in the boil. The process of pitching in hops during fermentation is dry-hopping. As American drinkers and brewers became enamored of the hop plant's citric and weedy and piney flavors, more hop infusions happened in the fermenter. Today's New England-style IPAs involve comparatively few boil hops in favor of multiple dry-hopping infusions.

Lesson 74: Drink a Selection of Single-Hop IPAs

Almost every beer in existence uses hops. Even the maltiest, yeasty, adjunct-heavy, barrel-aged ale has a hop presence. However, if you want to get a sense of how individual hop strains taste and smell, the IPA is where you go. For someone looking to become versed in the particular hop varieties, here are some single-hop options on the market!

Centennial

Centennial hops have a pleasing orange and lemon quality and lend a decent amount of bitterness. They exist in the same family as Cascade hops (of Sierra Nevada Pale Ale fame); Centennial is the sole hop in Bell's Two Hearted Ale and Founder's Centennial IPA.

Mosaic

Mosaic is one of the superstar hops of the East Coast IPA movement. Dank and fruity in equal measure, it's assertive enough to ride alone. Check it out in Pipework Brewing's Lizard King and Lone Pint Brewery's Yellow Rose.

Simcoe

If Centennial is the quintessence of fruit-forward hopping, Simcoe is the other end entirely. Floral and earthy, it's known for a cannabis-like nose. Single hop examples include Hoppyum IPA from Foothills Brewing and Peak Organic's Simcoe Spring Ale.

Nelson Sauvin

Nelson Sauvin is one of the smoothest flavoring hops around. Redolent of white wine and passion fruit, it is the showcase hop of Alpine Brewing's Nelson and Zeelander from Toppling Goliath.

Lesson 75: How does Yeast Affect the Taste of a Beer?

Yeast is an active ingredient in beer. As I've mentioned, it's the functional component that turns wort into full-strength beer. It also contributes mightily to flavor and aroma. It is certainly the case when we get into the realm of bottle-, cask-, or can-conditioned ales with live yeast continuing to do its work after packaging. Yeast can impart tartness, mustiness, sweetness, and spice to these beers. For an example, check out Firestone Walker' Double Barrel Ale, an homage to the cask-conditioned ale CAMRA champions. They ferment the Pale Ale with a traditional English Mild yeast, imparting and enhancing the caramel and floral character.

The Alchemist in Vermont, the brewer of the legendary Heady Topper Double IPA, imported an English strain nicknamed Conan. Brewers consider this yeast to be perfect for Juicy IPAs since it has a natural tropical fruit flavor.

Lesson 76: Learn the Components of Your Favorite Beer

With this information in the back of your head, I recommend that you try a fun experiment. Pick a craft beer that you've enjoyed in this process, then do some research to identify each of these components:

- Water source
- Malt bill
- Hop bill
- Yeast strain
- Any adjuncts, like coffee, cocoa nibs, fruit puree, etc.

It shouldn't take very long. Brewers are pretty forthcoming about their processes. It's part of cultivating a dedicated following! Their website might even mention where they get their water and any proprietary ingredients. Plus, beer-nerds can be an obsessive bunch. If you like a beer, I promise that someone on the internet has figured out how to brew a clone and posted the recipe.

To that end, you might want to take a crack at brewing a clone. If nothing else, you know the individual ingredients. Finally, knowing what malt and hop combinations appeal to you will give you something to latch onto when looking over an unfamiliar beer list.

Lesson 77: Review Some Beers on BeerAdvocate or Untappd

An employer once told me that the fastest way to learn something is to have to teach it. I've found that to be correct; I've also wondered how fair it is to the folks I'm teaching. Regardless, that adage can be tweaked a bit for our purposes.

The fastest way to discover your beer preferences is to write a review.

Websites like Untappd and BeerAdvocate (the former recently acquired the latter, incidentally) have excellent platforms to search, rate, and review almost any beer under the sun. When I started exclusively drinking craft beer in the early 2010s, I religiously logged the beers I drank on BeerAdvocate. They have a wonderful point system, where you can individually score appearance, aroma, taste, and mouthfeel. Whenever possible, I expounded on these categories with written reviews. It was one of the main ways I developed my vocabulary for describing and assessing beer. I emphatically recommend you give it a try!

Chapter Review

Any time you dig into a particular subculture - whether in art or music, sport or technology - you will want to familiarize yourself with its mechanics. Craft beer is no different. Here is a recap of the topics discussed.

- Water is an under-appreciated but pivotal component in a good beer. Brewers work hard to optimize the weight and pH of the water they use.
- Malts provide fermentable sugar to wort and lend weight, color, aroma, and taste to the beer.
- Hops can be used for both bittering and imparting flavors to a beer. When hops are added after the brew, while the beverage is fermenting, they can impart vibrant flavors and little bitterness. It is called dry-hopping.
- Yeast converts sugars to ethanol, but it also contributes quite a bit to the beer's flavor and aroma.
- When familiarizing yourself with the components of craft beer, try taking brewery tours, exploring brewing supply shops, and reviewing beers on BeerAdvocate and Untappd.

Chapter 7: Knowing the Variables

Okay, things are going to get crazy!

With so many craft brewers in America today, working from such sweeping, interlocking brewing traditions, they seem to refresh the game every few months. Some innovations catch drinkers' fancies for a season, then dissipate into the air. Others stand the test of time.

So, let's look at the variables that brewers, beer historians, chemists, technicians, and others have brought to craft beer.

Lesson 78: Taste Some Beers that Go Beyond the Hop Cone!

We have covered how hops are used quite a bit so far. If you've been paying attention (and I expect you have, if you've made it this far), it should be clear that hoppy beers dominate the craft beer scene right now. With that in mind, let's talk about some of the scientific advances made in hop science.

The most basic processed hop product, to start, is the pellet. Any homebrewer will recognize this item. It resembles a tiny green cork. Producers of these pellets dry hop cones, then grind them to a fine powder. They compress the powder into pellets, which are easier to store and generally more durable.

However, modern science pioneered new, efficient, massively popular products recently. In a process similar to the one used to synthesize keef from cannabis, labs are drawing out both bittering and flavor agents from hop cones. It includes hop oils, the use of which is typified by Sierra Nevada's Hop Hunter IPA. First released in 2014, this brew used fresh hop cones, but the brewer spiked them with distilled hop oil from Cascade and Centennial strains. The resulting IPA tasted taproom-fresh even after weeks on the shelf.

Hop Hunter was sort of a forerunner to a proliferation of super-fresh IPAs - mostly in tandem with the New England haze movement - that is dry-hopped, not with whole hops or pellets, but with dry lupulin powder. Often called Double Dry Hopped - or DDH - these ales pulse with a distilled hop flavor separated from attendant bitterness.

Some excellent examples of IPAs that make use of lupulin powder are:

- Bearded Iris - Chasing Rainbows
- Captain Lawrence - Powder Dreams
- Grimm Artisanal Ales - Lambo Door
- Hoof Hearted Brewing - I Must Look Like a Dork
- Long Trail Brewing - Over the Handlebars

Lesson 79: How are Lupulin Products Made?

At this point, you're probably wondering, what is lupulin? It's the operative component of the hop plant, containing enzymes that impart both flavor and bitterness. When brewers toss hop cones into boiling wort, it leeches these enzymes from the lupulin glands. This traditional form of hopping, however, can be inexact and risk infiltration of unintended flavors.

Washington-based hop lab Yakima Chief pioneered a process for extracting these glands and isolating the essential oils while minimizing bittering alpha acids and other potentially off-flavors. The resulting powder, called Cryo Hops, is like concentrated hop flavor. Brewers can pitch it in during fermentation for a cleaner, more vibrant, and more measurable flavor infusion.

As stated before, this process is not too far removed from the way CBD products are distilled from cannabis.

Lesson 80: Compare 2005 to 2020

We've talked at length about the shift in IPAs. It's easy to gloss over how broadly craft beer drinkers' tastes have shifted in a short period. At the turn of the twenty-first century, top-rated IPAs were face-meltingly bitter. An insane IBU (International Bitterness Unit) count was a badge of honor for many brewers. It elided an essential balance in these Pale Ales. Yes, they were palate-wrecking, but they also shocked you with an interplay of biscuit, resin, citrus, and yeast.

If you take a trip back to April 2005 in the Wayback Machine and load up the BeerAdvocate Top 100 Beers list, you'll be amazed, firstly, at how few Pale Ales are on there. Next, you might notice some fairly available brews on the list. Two IPAs that typify the high-bitterness fashion of the time are 3 Floyds' Dreadnaught (#12) and Alesmith IPA (#35). I recommend seeking those out. At least one should be on shelves near you.

Today, BeerAdvocate's Top Beers list is chock full of hazy IPAs, many only available in small distribution areas. Here are a few that might be in your area:

- Toppling Goliath's King Sue (#44)
- Lawson's Finest Liquid's Sip of Sunshine (#72)
- Surly Brewing's Axe Man (#246)

Do a side-by-side tasting of 2005 and 2020—Alesmith versus Axe Man, or Dreadnaught versus King Sue. You'll be amazed how the popular consensus of a tasty IPA has traveled. Personally, I love both traditions, the brutally bitter and the ethereally fruity. Which is your cup of tea ... or ale, as it were?

Lesson 81 - How Adjuncts Affect Beer

We could spend hundreds of pages discussing all the different things that can go into a beer. From the relatively mundane (coffee, cocoa nibs, blueberries) to the totally out-there (Earl Grey tea, whole donuts!), brewers are continually experimenting with adjunct additions to their brews.

Adjuncts fundamentally shift about every metric on a beer. Fruit and candied items add sugar to fermenting wort, which will boost the final ABV. If you add berries to a Berliner Weisse or Farmhouse Ale, you might produce a pink or purple product. Lactose will thicken the body of ale, and dark roast coffee will dominate the nose.

These are just a few examples of how adjuncts affect beer. The variables are countless, and these days you can experience a lot of variables. Adjuncts have always been a part of brewing, but now they are seemingly taking over!

Lesson 82: Try some Beers with Cherries on Top

For the sake of brevity - and so we don't go totally off the rails - let's look at one specific adjunct. I'm selecting cherries because they have found their way into many, many different beer styles over the years. So, let's dig into how this one adjunct affects various beers:

Sour Brown Ale - Lost Abbey's Red Poppy

This San Marcos brewer has made some of the most acclaimed sours in America. This brown ale ages on oak with sour cherries. The resulting ale is stout, intensely tart, and wildly carbonated.

Lambic - Allagash Brewing's Coolship Cerise

Allagash Brewing in Portland, Maine, distributes their stable beers widely, but their limited coolship Sours are rare. This Kriek-style ale incorporates local cherries. It's puckery sour with a champagne finish—deceptively light for an 8.1% ABV.

Stout - Bell's Brewing's Cherry Stout

Bell's Brewing in Kalamazoo is one of the truly exceptional generalist brewers. They produce great brews in every style, and this is one of their more peculiar regular offerings. A mild 7% Stout melds potent dark chocolate notes with the sweet tang of Michigan cherry-juice.

Farmhouse Ale - Hill Farmstead Brewery's Flora with Cherries and Raspberries

Florence is Hill Farmstead's year-round wheated Farmhouse Ale. Flora is this ale aged in wine barrels. Now and then, Shaun Hill's team pitches some fruit in with Flora. This multi-adjunct variant pours the color of Welch's cranberry juice and pops like a fruity Italian soda!

Berliner Weisse - North Coast Brewing's Berliner Weisse: Tart Cherry

Light as a feather and delectably funky, this California brewer's Berliner incorporates the same Michigan region's cherries as Bell's. With a puckery sweetness and super-easy 4.1% ABV, you could drink these all afternoon.

Lesson 83: Pair a Coffee Beer with Breakfast!

I'm not suggesting you make a habit of drinking in the morning here, sometimes – when you don't have to work or drive or operate machinery – a beer can be the perfect complement to a stack of waffles. In particular, I'm talking about Coffee Stouts. Craft brewers often forge relationships with local coffee roasters. Goose Island works with Intelligentsia. Against the Grain works with Heine Brothers. The point is you are likely to experience some top-tier beans with a high-end Coffee Stout. I recommend Sump from Perennial Artisan Ales in St. Louis. A straight-up, no-frills Imperial Stout spiked with Scott Carey & Co. Coffee; this ale is aggressive as a double espresso with none of the attendant acid. Fair warning, though. It's an unforgiving 11.5% ABV and comes packaged in 750 mL bottles.

Lesson 84: Drink Your Dessert

Just as you can start your day with a Strong Dark Ale, you can end it that way as well. Dessert Stouts - aka

Pastry Stouts - is one of the most ascendant sub-styles in craft beer today; beer purists tend to shake their heads at these milk-shake thick, candy-tasting, booze-heavy ales, but there's something undeniably alluring about them.

The definition of Pastry Stout is a bit nebulous. I'm inclined to paraphrase Potter Stewart's famous aphorism about pornography: "I know it when I taste it." There's a laundry list of adjuncts that make frequent appearances in these beers: cocoa nibs, coconut, vanilla, coffee, marshmallow, almonds, maple syrup, and pecans. On the crazier side, you might find peanut butter, peanut butter cups, graham crackers, bananas, caramel, Nutella, or Nilla wafers.

I tend to think of the Pastry originators as variants of seasonal Barrel-Aged Stouts. These immediately leap to mind:

- **Goose Island's 2013 Proprietor's Bourbon County Brand Stout** - the first "Prop" vintage of Goose Island's extra-strong Bourbon County series was aged in Rye Barrels with toasted coconut. Devotees described it as a boozy liquid Mounds bar.
- **The Bruery's Chocolate Rain and Grey Monday** - Orange County's The Bruery already had one of the biggest, thickest Stouts globally with 20% ABV Black Tuesday. These two variations went even further. Chocolate Rain added cocoa and vanilla beans, while Grey Monday added hazelnuts.

Today, some of the hippest, gnarliest stouts around go further. Angry Chair Brewing in Tampa makes the much-desired Imperial German Chocolate Cupcake Stout. Down the peninsula, Miami's J. Wakefield Brewing has It Was All A Dream, a Stout loaded with coffee, coconut, and vanilla, then aged in maple syrup bourbon barrels. In Colorado, the multi-award-winning Weldwerks Brewing has the Medianoche series, a Barrel-Aged Stout they load up with a rotating list of adjuncts. My favorite of these is probably Medianoche - Peanut Butter Cup.

Lesson 85: The Brewer that Let Drinkers Make a Personal Adjunct Stout

As you might imagine, the process of loading down a Pastry Stout with confectionery adjuncts is pricy, arduous, and perilous. A rogue bacterium on some coconut or a peanut butter cup could spoil a whole batch. Barrel-aging is even more expensive and time-consuming. So, as much as your average homebrewer would love to try their hand at a Pastry Stout, it's pretty impractical.

Enter: Prairie Artisan Ales in Tulsa, Oklahoma. Prairie won acclaim since opening 2012 for its innovative dark ales. One of the first widely-available Mexican Stouts (i.e., a Stout brewed with coffee, vanilla, and chili peppers) was Prairie's Bomb! In 2017, Prairie came up with a crazy notion; the Prairie Dawg Member program. For a cool $3,600, any member (or, as often, group of members) could essentially reserve a bourbon or rum barrel's worth of Stout. Members could elect to add as many as three adjuncts and pick their beer name, which Prairie would print labels for and submit to the Alcohol and Tobacco Tax and Trade Bureau. Each barrel yielded about eight and a half kegs worth of finished beer. It was a bananas program, with such member-created entries as Scoop Dawg (vanilla, cocoa nibs, and strawberry) and Buford T. Justice (vanilla, coconut, and maple syrup).

Lesson 86: Spirit Barrels and Craft Beer

By this point, I am sure you've noticed that a lot of craft beer is barrel-aged. Indeed, the term has a lot of different meanings. Many beers are aged on wood. Before stainless steel fermenting tanks become industry standard, giant wood foeders were the norm.

When you hear the term Barrel-Aged these days, the beer in question was normally aged in spirit barrels. The most popular spirit cask for aging is Bourbon, but you will also find Brandy, Rum, Rye, Gin, Tequila, and others. Aging on spent spirit barrels will naturally impart flavors of both wood and the particular liquor. Also, these barrels are saturated with booze (what distillers call the Devil's Cut). So, spirit barrel-aging also boosts the ABV of a beer.

Imperial Stouts fare particularly well in spirit barrels as their full body and robust flavor profile can stand up against a bold, boozy whiskey or brandy. There are quite a few popular Barrel-Aged Barleywines like Firestone Walker's Sucaba, Pelican Brewing's Mother of All Storms, and Anchorage Brewing's A Deal with the Devil. Other styles that see barrel-aging a lot:

Wheatwine (Bruery's White Chocolate), Quadrupel (Sun King's Velvet Fog), and Tripel (Captain Lawrence's Golden Delicious)

Lesson 87: Why are Bourbon Barrels So Prevalent in Craft Beer?

What makes a bourbon, officially? It's not like Champagne, where it needs to be made in Bourbon County, Kentucky. Fine bourbons are made in Colorado, New York, and beyond. There are rules, though. For one, the mash must be composed of at least 51% corn. Another rule is that the whiskey must be aged in first-use, charred oak barrels. This rule accounts for its dark hue and the complex flavor drawn from components in the wood.

So, bourbon distillers only use their casks one time. Once upon a time, they couldn't give away their spent barrels. A Kentuckian myself, I have an in-law whose uncle used to travel the world looking for any business that might take casks off his whiskey-making employer's hands. He almost convinced Tabasco in the 1970s, but the deal fell through.

Oh, how times have changed!

In 1992, Goose Island aged an Imperial Stout in spent Jim Beam barrels. The resulting beer, Bourbon County Brand Stout, changed American beer forever. Today, distillers can make a decent profit from their used barrels. Brewers, vintners, syrup makers, and, yes, hot sauce producers covet this boozy wood. One of the highest-ranked Stouts in America, Founders Brewing's Canadian Breakfast Stout, is aged in a third-use barrel. The coffee-chocolate Stout ages on bourbon barrels that were later used to age maple syrup!

Tip 88: Try a Base Beer and its Barrel-Aged Version

Curious how a spirit barrel affects a base beer? It's not always easy to make a comparison. Some brewers are cagey about what base they use. Founder's KBS might derive from their Imperial Stout, but they've never confirmed that. Some brewers create a Cuvee of different beers for their base. For example, Bell's Brewing's lovely Black Note Stout uses a combination of their Expedition Stout and their Double Cream Stout.

If you want to compare a base beer to its BA version, though, I recommend hitting up Ten FIDY from Oskar Blues in Lyons, Colorado. Ten FIDY is a gargantuan devil's food cake of a Stout. Oskar Blues broke with convention in 2007 when they released the Stout in cans rather than bottles. In 2016, they broke the mold again by releasing Barrel-Aged Ten FIDY in 22-ounce tallboy cans.

It is one of those funny beers that mellows a little when coming into contact with bourbon cask wood. The soy-saucy, biting edges of the base Stout gets sanded down from the whiskey's caramel and vanilla. It may take some doing, but I recommend securing both of these beers and giving them a try, side-by-side.

Lesson 89: While You're at it, Compare Multiple Spirit Barrels with the Same Base Beer

Truckee, California's FiftyFifty Brewing, makes a lot of fine beers, but if you know them for one thing, it's probably their Eclipse Stout Series. You can't miss them in a bottle shop, a line of dark-brown glass bombers that would be identical if not for the spectrum of different-colored waxes cascading down each neck. Most shops carrying the Eclipse series post some sort of color rubric, so you know which distiller each wax color denotes: Four Roses, Elijah Craig, Booker's, Basil Hayden, High West, and on and on and on.

To start, the base of all Eclipse beers is the FiftyFifty's Totality, a honey-infused Imperial Stout. The brewery ages this Stout in barrels from multiple distillers. They add vanilla to some barrels or coconut or cherries. They have brewery-only vintages, too, from super-rare casks like Pappy Van Winkle. This series is an excellent opportunity to see how different spirit types affect the same ale. I've had about a dozen Eclipse Beers over the years, and Buffalo Trace is my favorite. That's odd since plain-jane BT is not a bourbon I particularly love.

Fair warning: Eclipse isn't cheap. Four bombs will probably run you about a hundred bucks. But it's money well spent for a little extra, shall we say, wisdom.

Lesson 90: Try Utopias, the Mother of All Barrel-Aged Beers

In 1992, Boston Beer Company released a huge whiskey-barrel-aged German-style ale called Triple Bock. At 17.5% ABV, it was just about the strongest American beer ever made to that point. It was also the beginning of a multi-year barrel-aging experiment that continues to this day.

In 2000, after two more vintages of Triple Bock, Boston Beer created the next iteration, Millennium Ale. Using the same spirit barrels as Triple Bock, Jim Koch's brewery team blended the Bock, plus other cellared ales. Millennium, or MMM, was lighter in color and ABV than Triple Bock, with lots of caramel, fig, and cherry notes.

The experiment continued in 2002 with Utopias. This blended variation on MMM, aged yet again in whiskey barrels, clocked in at 21% ABV. From there, Boston Beer released a new Utopias vintage 2005, then every two years after. Each release, the prior Utopias is blended with an increasing range of barrel-aged ales. The alcohol threshold keeps rising. Initially, all Utopias came out of Buffalo Trace casks. Still, in the intervening two decades, that expanded to include other Bourbons, as well as - to name a few - Port, Sherry, Cognac, Calvados, Madeira, Rum, Aquavit, and Scotch.

The first Utopias vintage I tried was 2013, a blend of Bourbon and Port ales, combined with an Abbey Ale aged on fragrant Hungarian wood. It was a head-spinning 28% ABV with the viscous quality of new motor oil. It is neither a surprising nor especially original observation, but it resembled port-wine or brandy more than beer. Despite being re-fermented with champagne yeast, it's mostly devoid of carbonation. Boston Beer packages it in a beautiful, resealable 25-ounce ceramic bottle shaped like a copper brew kettle.

Utopias is delicious, though, and every beer lover should try it. It retains between $200 and $250 per bottle.

Lesson 91: Do an Experiment in Component Parts

I have done this experiment before, and it's a lot of fun! I'll walk you through an example, but you can do it with any adjunct-heavy and/or barrel-aged brew.

Let's say you snag a bottle of the aforementioned It Was All A Dream Stout from J. Wakefield. Firstly, congrats! It's an unbelievable brew. Now, let's look at what goes into this beer. First, the base is J. Wakefield's Big Poppa, which involves:

- A Base Imperial Stout, probably something like La Nada
- Mostra Coffee
- Vanilla
- Coconut

Then, this adjunct stout is aged in a bourbon cask with maple syrup. Here are some distillers we know supply J. Wakefield:

- Willet
- Belle Meade
- Copper and Kings
- Joseph Magnus
- One Eight
- Peerless

Before cracking It Was All A Dream, how about enjoying some vanilla-and-coconut pancakes slathered in Michigan maple syrup, accompanied by a cup of Mostra Philippines Benguet Farmer's Coffee. Then, have a half-pain of La Nada and a nip of one of the bourbons listed above.

You've tried an approximation of all the components of the Pastry Stout you're about to enjoy!

For good measure, maybe put on the *Ready to Die* album too.

Chapter Review

As you can see, the craft beer world is more than just malts and hops. Brewers today are embracing a wide variety of innovations and ingredients. And the examples listed above are just scratching the surface! To recap:

- As hazy, low-bitterness, high-flavor IPAs grow in popularity, brewers turn to lupulin products that extract hop enzymes and concentrate them into powder and oil.

- Adjuncts have always been popular, but today, brewers fill their beers with all sorts of unexpected, flavorful items.
- Pastry Stouts are on the rise! Today, you can find giant Dark Ales loaded down with chocolate, vanilla, peanut butter, coconut, hazelnut spread, and countless other sinful delicacies.
- Distilleries – especially Bourbon producers – sell their spent barrels to craft brewers to age strong ales. These casks intensify the ABV, taste, smell, and body of the already-burly beer.
- With all these technological advances, new methods, and esoteric additions, craft brewers are pushing what beer can be.

Chapter 8: Navigating the Craft Beer Hype Train

I'll begin this final chapter with a bit of a warning.

Craft beer can begin as a diversion, grow into a passion, and curdle into a bit of an obsession.

In some of my prior writing, I have likened American beer nerds to folks that collected Beanie Babies back in the day. For those lucky enough not to recall that unfortunate trend in the late 1990s and early 2000s, the Ty brand plush figurines' rising popularity gave way to a massive buying frenzy, speculation, and, eventually, forgeries. The culture, writ large, somehow convinced itself that these things, which were just cute beanbags, were going to become collectors' items of real value.

It's cooled a bit, but craft beer can have comparable excesses. There are "real value" boards and secondary markets and, yes, forgeries. I'm not joking. A few years ago, a guy in Iowa was caught filling and recapping bottles from Toppling Goliath Stouts that sell on the secondary market for hundreds of dollars. He then conned beer traders into sending him equally-valued beers in exchange for recapped bottles, now filled with some random ale. The trading community went nuts in productive and unproductive ways. Online beer boards indexed the duped traders and sent them consolation bottles, which was great. These boards also outed the malefactor to his employer, which is more ethically dubious.

Okay, don't get freaked out. That was an extreme example, meant to illustrate the obsessive length to which craft beer folks can take this interest. If you enjoy craft beer - even if you trade it and get involved on the fan forums - you probably won't get caught in a fake bottle trading scam.

What might happen - what's happened to me more times than I care to admit - is you could end up stepping into a bottle shop on a whim and end up spending a hundred bucks on beer.

So, here are my final tips. My goal here is to show you how to enjoy this American beer scene to the fullest without getting overwhelmed by the hype around it.

Lesson 92: Top 10 Lists Can be a Fun Guide, but They Aren't Gospel

As I've mentioned before, craft beer is not exactly cheap. It's natural when spending a considerable amount of coin for you to want the best. And there is no shortage of Best Beer lists out there. Indeed, both RateBeer and BeerAdvocate have constantly-refreshing top-rated beer lists on their sites. I remember sliding into the BeerAdvocate list in 2014, right when I was starting out trading beer and scouring bottle shops. Pretty much every beer in the Top Ten was only available in its immediate locality or a super-limited distribution window.

Checking in today, I see that, if anything, this has only intensified. Six of the BeerAdvocate Top Ten are once-a-year releases, and only one of them is available outside of its brewery. That one, incidentally, is Heady

Topper, the progenitor of the East Coast IPA. It's available year-round in part of Vermont.

Scrolling down, I find a few in the Top 20 - Pliny the Elder, Canadian Breakfast Stout, Fundamental Observation - that see out-of-state distribution. The point is these lists tend to hew toward limited releases. They also skew hard toward IPAs and Imperial Stouts. I'm not saying that you shouldn't look at them. They give you a good sense of where craft beer is headed. But you probably won't find your new favorite go-to beer there.

Lesson 93: Check Local Websites and Periodicals with Top 10 Lists for Your Region

On the other hand, a Best Beer list tailored to your region is a goldmine. Is there an Alt weekly in your area? I guarantee they've run a local beer listicle in the last year. Dip into their online archives, and you will find some top-tier brews you can drink in your area. If you're in a major city, Time Out Magazine always has a beer list brewing, so to speak. BeerAdvocate's Top Beers Lists can also be filtered by region and state, so that should help your search. I always check those filtered lists when I'm taking a vacation.

I will also note that you can identify world-class beers in more-or-less wide distribution fairly easily. One way is to check BeerAdvocate's Beers of Fame List. It is a rundown of top-rated brews that are over 15 years old. Essentially, it filters out the flavors-of-the-week. You can also go to archive.org and load up RateBeer or BeerAdvocate lists from years past.

Many beers you find on archived lists or Beers of Fame will still be out-of-market for you, but many will be on shelves and taps in your neck of the woods. See, yesterday's "white whale" is today's dusty shelf beer. If you had told me, even five years ago, that I'd walk into a grocery store with KBS, Zombie Dust, and Sip of Sunshine in the cooler, I'd have called you nuts. But here we are!

Lesson 94: Find Good Local Options that are Comparable to Top-Rated Rarities.

I've said it before, but I'll say it again: you should seek the advice of beer professionals. Whether it's a taproom worker, a bartender, or a shop employee, they can provide you with excellent local and widely-distributed options. Moreover, many of them have tried those super-rare, highly-rated beers you might be curious about, and they can recommend readily-available options that are comparable. Again, there's nothing wrong with having a rare beer bucket list. However, you have the good fortune of living in an era where world-class beer is native to every American square-mile. Tap someone who can help you find it!

Lesson 95: Don't Sit on Beer!

There's a long-simmering argument among beer drinkers about whether you can cellar beer. Some categorically state that you should never age beer. I think there's a bit more nuance in the question of a beer cellar. Here are some points I believe are valid:

- More often than not, beer should be consumed fresh. Hops and adjuncts fade pretty quickly. Oxygen infiltrates packaging, degrading the product and leading to off-flavors.
- Beer doesn't become toxic, but it can turn. Anyone who's opened an older Stout and tasted balsamic vinaigrette can attest to that. The longer you sit on a beer, the more likely a tiny agent will infect it.
- Some beers do better with age than others. High-ABV styles like Stouts and Barleywines can develop interestingly. So, too, can live-culture sours like Lambics.

I have a few beers that I love sitting on for months and years to see how they develop. None rely too hard on hopping or ingredients like coffee and vanilla. So, why am I saying you shouldn't sit on beer? Candidly, if you're just starting to explore craft beer, by definition, you haven't tried a lot of beers. So, you won't be able to tell the difference between, say, a fresh or an aged Plead the Fifth Stout. Drink the beer you buy. Brewers always make more.

Lesson 96: Seek Out Beer Festivals

Want to try some out-of-market beer? Want to share your newfound love of craft with some like-minded new friends? Are you interested in expanding your style horizons? Beer festivals are an excellent way to sample lots of exciting brews and acquaint yourself with the broader brewing and drinking community. You can drink scores of excellent, unfamiliar brews in easy two-ounce tasters. Here are a few of the coolest festivals out there, in my opinion:

The Great American Beer Festival (Denver, CO)

The granddaddy of American beer-fests. This US equivalent to the Great British Beer Festival began in 1982. It includes the preeminent beer awards competition, and in recent years, nearly one thousand breweries attended.

Oregon Brewers Festival (Portland, OR)

One of the country's longest-running festivals, this outdoor summer shindig features about a hundred brewers from the Beaver State.

Festival of Barrel-Aged Beers (Chicago, IL)

Since 2003, FOBAB has awarded medals for great wood-aged beers and hosted one hell of a rowdy festival. It is the largest gathering of barrel-aged brews.

Pastrytown and Green City (Brooklyn, NY)

Other Half Brewing hosts two festivals dedicated to the dual ascendant styles in contemporary craft. In late winter, they hold Pastrytown, a celebration of the boozy, sweet Pastry Stout. In the summer, there's Green City, dedicated to the New England IPA.

Dark Lord Day (Munster, IN)

Limited beer releases can be an excuse for a good party. Three Floyds Brewing's annual Dark Lord release is remarkable for its excess. Held in the early summer, the release of this extra-strong Stout combines with exclusive guest brewery pours, impromptu bottle sharing, and a heavy metal music lineup. It's big, brash, and more than a little gnarly.

Fresh Fest (Pittsburgh, PA)

Founded in 2018 by Drinking Partners Podcast hosts Day Bracey and Ed Bailey and Black Brew Culture founder Mike Potter, this festival focuses on black-owned craft breweries. A combined block party, concert, tap-pour, and professional conference - there's nothing else quite like Fresh Fest.

Lesson 97: Dip Your Toe in Beer Trading

For a community that's already insular and prone to hype-chasing, beer trading can be especially intense. Trade boards feature odd abbreviations that resemble World War II codes. Limited beer released on the other side of the country will inspire mad trading frenzies. Traders argue relative value like hagglers in an ancient marketplace.

With all that said, trading is also bloody awesome! For someone getting into the craft, it can be a way to try beers from all over the country. Here are a few quick tips:

- You can find trading boards on both BeerAdvocate and Untappd. Trading also takes place on Facebook, Instagram, and Reddit.
- A great starting point is "Locals for Locals" trading. You post the breweries available exclusively in your area, and folks will offer their local brews in exchange. You can then agree on styles and send each other a beer package.
- If you want, you can try your hand at negotiating trades for rare or limited brews. Just be aware this can be competitive.

Lesson 98: Alternatives to Trading

If you are looking for another option for trying unfamiliar or rare beers and don't want to get into the involved and expensive world of trading, there are other internet-aided options out there. For example:

- Beer Raffles - Beer aficionados will often offer rare bottles for a raffle in exchange for charity donations. It's a great way to score a great brew potentially, plus you'll be helping a good cause.
- Beer it Forward - this goes by many names, but essentially, it's a beer chain letter. One person ships a box of beer to another person. That person sends beer to the next, and on and on. The group agrees to a price limit, and a central organizer determines the shipment order. Then, participants can post photos of the incredible beers they get!

- Competitions - Are you a fantasy sports fan? There are plenty of leagues out there; here, team owners put up beer instead of cash, and the playoff winner gets the haul. The same goes for NCAA brackets and Super Bowl boxes.

Lesson 99: Host a Tasting of Bottle Share

As I've been describing these beer-sharing options, you might think all beer-nerds sit in darkened rooms in front of a computer, trading ales. Believe it or not, many beer-lovers venture out into the real world and engage in face-to-face human interaction! Having an in-person bottle share or beer tasting is unbelievably fun. Bars and breweries often host these events, inviting patrons to bring a special bottle to share with the group.

You can host one of these shares in the comfort of your own home, too. Just be sure to include a decent spread of food and water to temper the alcohol consumption. You can also set a theme for the night. Maybe you just do Porters or Wheat Beers. What about choosing an ingredient and challenging everyone to find a highly-rated ale that incorporates it? If you have homebrewers in the group, have them bring homemade wares. The options are virtually limitless. Plus, you get to enjoy an evening with new and established pals, discussing and debating your shared love of beer!

Lesson 100: Set a Limit on Your Beer Consumption

I do not doubt that once you start sampling what American craft beer has to offer, you will fall in love. In my experience, many folks that get into craft beer have to re-assess their finances after a while. I certainly did!

So, I will offer this humble suggestion. Please approach your budgetary commitment to beer the same way you approach your health. Just as it's unhealthy to house ten beers in a night, it's unsustainable to buy ten bombers of craft beer every week. To begin with, you probably won't drink everything you purchase. You'll end up sitting on beer that will deteriorate. Beer traders are especially prone to over-extend their finances because every expensive, appealing beer is potential trade fodder. These days, I never buy a beer unless I can specifically picture when I drink it. This one will be good with tomorrow's dinner. That one will be a great Friday night treat.

Yet, just as we occasionally have a few too many at the bar, we'll sometimes go overboard with our beer acquisitions. One screw-up isn't the end of the world. Just be sure to set your craft beer limits and stay cognizant of your spending.

Lesson 101: Get Drinking!

There you have it, friend. You have a pretty comprehensive primer on the history, evolution, and artistry behind craft beer. I sincerely hope that you found these tips, lessons, and fun facts both informative and entertaining. My dearest hope is that they got you excited to explore the wide, wild, weird world of American craft beer.

So, get going! There are so many exciting brews out there. Pick something new up today and open it with a friend, a loved one, or just in front of the TV. Beer may not be the answer to all life's uncertainty, but it makes the journey more enjoyable!

Chapter Review

- Best Beer lists can offer a great snapshot of the wider craft beer scene, but the beers are often limited and hard to find.
- Seek out local Best Beer lists from the web of Alt Weekly periodicals. You can also ask beer professionals for their thoughts.
- Seek out beer festivals like The Great American Beer Festival, Festival of Barrel-Aged Beers, Green City, and Fresh Fest
- Start with Beer Trading by exchanging Locals for Locals. You can also participate in Beer Raffles, Beer it Forward, Beer Fantasy Leagues, Bottle Shares, and Tastings.
- Don't go overboard! It's easy to buy more beer than you can reasonably drink. Moderation is the name of the game.

Top 10 Popular Craft Beers for Beginners

There are thousands of craft beers on the market these days, which is incredible! However, if you just began exploring independent brewers, here are ten popular beers to get you started.

Please note: I've tried to choose a decent range of styles here. I also stuck to brewers that have been around a few years and fall within the popular consensus of quality. It isn't a comprehensive "Best Beers" list. It's just what I'd recommend to someone who wants a broad survey of great craft beers.

1. **90 Minute IPA from Dogfish Head Brewing (Rehoboth Beach, Delaware)** - A ground-breaker in the American IPA. In the late 1990s, Sam Calagione's brewing team used a tabletop football game to rattle a continuous flow of hops into boiling wort. For ninety minutes, a steady rain of hop cones tumbled down. The 90 Minute IPA was born. A muscular 9% ABV, crackling with bitterness, bursting with both bready malt and citric hops - this is what a hardcore first-wave IPA should taste like. It's abrasive as hell but undeniably delicious.
2. **Parabola from Firestone Walker Brewing (Paso Robles, California)** - This is a masterclass on what an elegantly-crafted Stout, a bourbon barrel, and time can create. With so many Barrel-Aged Stouts on the market, you shouldn't overlook this no-frills exemplar. Aged for one year on Bourbon-y

charred oak, this 14% ale looks like spent engine oil and tastes like whiskey-soaked dark chocolate, coated in Nutella. If that sounds busy to you, it somehow isn't. Parabola manages to contain everything wonderful about spirit-cask beers without overstating its case. Truly magical.

3. **Fat Tire from New Belgium Brewing (Fort Collins, Colorado)** - Upon its 1991 introduction as New Belgium's flagship beer, this slightly sweet, herbal Amber Ale took up permanent residence in Colorado and beyond. Its popularity is even more impressive considering the precipitous decline in popularity for Ambers. New Belgium was the fourth highest-selling craft brewer in America in 2019, and Fat Tire is still its biggest seller. It is a direct rebuttal to that hipster-ish opinion that if something is popular, it must be trash.

4. **Sorachi Ace Saison from Brooklyn Brewery (Brooklyn, New York)** - In 2009, Garrett Oliver, the beer oracle of the Five Boroughs, all but reinvented the Saison with this magnificent specimen. Fermented first with Belgian ale yeast, then re-fermented with Champagne yeast, this Farmhouse Ale is dry-hopped with the eponymous Japanese hop, a noble-ish cone with lemony and herbal notes. Sorachi Ace Saison was way ahead of the curve on farmhouse beers, lighter than many of its kin but still complex and flavorful.

5. **Heady Topper from The Alchemist (Waterbury, Vermont)** - When The Alchemist's Waterbury brewpub was all but destroyed in 2011 by flooding connected with Hurricane Irene, they scaled back the ambition

of their operations. They focused for years only on brewing and canning their Double IPA, Heady Topper. Within a couple of years, American beer drinkers overwhelmed the small town searching for this invigorating concoction. Folks call it the forerunner of the New England IPA, but I find that it straddles the line between East Coast and West. Heady Topper is bracingly bitter, but that hoppy bite immediately subsides with a bouquet of grass and grapefruit. It's unfiltered but not hazy. Heady, in the end, is just one-of-a-kind.

6. **King Titus from Maine Beer Company (Portland, Maine)** - Any number of Maine Beer Company ales could be on this list. Certainly, they've contributed two or three outstanding IPAs to the craft beer oeuvre, but King Titus deserves special commendation as an almost peerless American Porter. A burly 7.5% ABV, Titus boasts a grain bill with not only Caramel, Munich, and Chocolate Malts but also flaked oats and wheat. The result is silky smooth and pulsing with coffee and baker's chocolate notes. Even more surprising is the woodsy, lemony hop presence. It is a magnificent example of a sorely overlooked style.

7. **Dancing Man from New Glarus Brewing (New Glarus, Wisconsin)** - New Glarus is an unprepossessing Midwestern town, and its brewery is just as low-key. It's truly impressive, then, that New Glarus Brewing is such a dominant presence in American beer. Hell, it's only available in Wisconsin! Their seasonal Hefeweizen Dancing Man is something to behold, though. The wheat presence of this

surprisingly-strong lager is delectable. While other wheat beers are estery and spicy, Dancing Man explodes with cloves, citrus, and cotton candy. It's dangerously easy-drinking and pairs perfectly with sweet or savory meals.

8. **Bigfoot Ale from Sierra Nevada Brewing (Chico, California)** - There are so many fine American Barleywines out there, but nothing quite like Bigfoot. In a world where so many strong ales are tossed into spirit barrels, there's something so pure about this hop-inundated, deep red 9.6% behemoth. It's one of the few American beers that are undeniably cellar-able. I genuinely cannot say which is more satisfying to me: a fresh, harrowingly bitter forest-floor Bigfoot; or a ten-year-old cognac and caramel Bigfoot. Best just to buy a six-pack and set half of it aside.

9. **Speedway Stout from Alesmith Brewing (San Diego, California)** - When done correctly, coffee can push a good Stout recipe into the stratosphere; it is somehow the strongest and the most mutable adjunct. One of the first beers to show this potential was Speedway Stout. There's nothing subtle or delicate about Speedway. It's malted-milk thick, impenetrably black, strapping in flavor, aroma, and booze. So, it's always a shock to experience how elegantly the dark-roast coffee plays off a grain base full of toffee and date. Speedway is available nationwide, and year-round is amazing. For extra credit, seek out their Vietnamese Coffee variant, which is somehow even better!

10. **Supplication from Russian River Brewing (Santa Rosa, California)** - There

are so many Sour Ales in America, and they are brewed in various ways. So, I think it best to highlight one that is widely available, unimpeachably made, and utterly delicious. Russian River Brewing is among the most lauded craft brewers ever, and Supplication is one of their finest sours. A dark ale aged extensively in California Pinot Noir barrels with Cherries, Supplication ferments with Brettanomyces, Lactobacillus, and Pediococcus. The resulting ale is medium-bodied, medium-strength, and shimmering with sweet-tart fruit notes. It is a pitch-perfect intro to the world of modern Fruited Sours.

11. One final thing to bear in mind: not every brewer distributes everywhere in the country. Also, not all beers are available year-round. Dancing Man and Heady Topper are only available in their home states. Supplication and King Titus are distributed, but some areas won't have nearby access. Pretty much every other beer on the list is available nationwide. However, Parabola and Bigfoot are seasonal releases.

Drink on, my friends! I'm confident you'll find a couple of new favorites on this list.

Frequently Asked Questions

If you're just getting into craft beer, you will no doubt have some questions. I hope that the preceding 101 Tips, Lessons, and Fun Facts cleared a lot of them up. However, here are a few FAQs that will fill in some gaps:

Where are the best stores to buy craft beer?

We have discussed how local breweries and bottle shops are a great place to buy the freshest and best-curated craft beer throughout this book. Many also offer growler and crowler carry-out options for draft beer. Large beverage chains like Total Wine or Binny's are excellent sources, as well. A lot of grocery chains are investing in extensive craft beer selection, as well. Some great options are:

- Whole Foods
- Costco
- Wegmans
- DeCicco's
- Giant Eagle
- Fred Meyer

Why isn't a specific beer available in my area?

Unfortunately, not all craft beers are available nationwide. You have to remember that every brewery is effectively a startup. In most regions, a new brewery begins by pouring their wares in the taproom and shipping kegs to local bars. Over time, they normally start packaging in bottles and cans. Even then, they will likely stay local since beer distribution is such a considerable cost. Getting regulatory approvals and setting up distributor pipelines are arduous tasks, and breweries need to do them for every new state.

Even if a brewery has the financial and workforce capabilities to expand distribution to other states, it may elect not to do so. After all, once a keg or case of beer leaves the brewery, quality control is out of the brewer's hands. Many breweries place strong caveats on their vendors – requiring constant refrigeration, enforcing sell-by dates – but others choose to limit their footprint instead.

Why is craft beer so expensive?

There is, to be clear, a wide range of prices for the large category of craft beer. One bottle of Sour Ale might cost thirty dollars, but a twelve-pack of Session IPA will be fifteen. A recent analysis by HuffPost determined that distribution and retailer markup comprise half the cost of a craft beer. Remember, most craft brewers don't distribute through the cheaper channels of macro-brewers. And retailers know that craft beer drinkers are willing to pay more for a superior product. That markup usually is as much as the brewery's production cost per bottle.

Still, the ingredients play a significant role too. Bud Light uses incredibly cheap adjuncts like rice to replace malted barley. So, there's almost no comparison between that type of beer and even something like Boston Lager. Once you start getting into ales brewed with imported vanilla beans and aged in Bourbon casks that cost brewers $100 each, the margin begins to make sense.

Can craft beer go bad?

In short, no. Beer – unless someone tampers with it – will not go bad in the same way milk does. The fermentation process, you may recall, was used to render water potable. So, no matter how long your craft beer sits and collects dust, it won't become toxic. With that being said, it will probably get staler and flatter. The hops in your IPA will fade. Your Coffee Stout will start to taste a little like cardboard. Refrigeration will slow this deterioration, but it won't halt it in its tracks. So, drink that beer soon after you buy it!

How can I find out when a certain beer is coming out?

I recommend following your favorite breweries on Facebook, Twitter, and Instagram. Their marketing teams will flood social media with each new release. If you want to plan, though, you can look for a release schedule on the brewer's website. If all else fails, fire off an email to the brewery. Your local beer-vendor might have some insight, as well. Stores often receive warnings of upcoming releases.

It seems like the really good beers sell out immediately. How do I find them before they get bought up?

Once you get into craft beer, you find that some beer releases can look like an Hermes sample sale or a Yeezy sneaker drop. Lines around the corner!

I remember waiting in line for Other Half Brewing's 2nd Anniversary IPA release, a collaboration with the trendy Trillium Brewing. On a frigid Saturday morning, hundreds of us queued hours in advance of the taproom's opening. Across the street, some passersby asked, "What you guys in line for?" We replied, "Beer!"

They looked at each other and replied, "Is it free?"

The point is, beer-nerds will do next-level dumb stuff to get a limited release. I'm talking, dragging your elderly uncle in to get a second allotment or following the distributor's truck around town. Sometimes, you just can't compete with that. However, some tactics can help your odds and still allow you to look at yourself in the mirror without shame. First is the old mantra: talk to your local beer seller! They know when the super-rare item is dropping. They have to plan the exact moment to begin selling it, so there's no mob scene. They can give you the details. BeerMenus is an app where restaurants, bars, and beer-sellers can update their available brews in real-time. Not every town uses BeerMenus, but if yours does, you should follow that hard-to-find beer and get updates when a business adds it to their menu.

Why are some beers only available on draft?

The packaging is expensive. For most brewers, it's their single largest overhead expense. So, it's a big decision to create a label for a new beer (which also must be approved by the Tax and Trade Bureau) and package it for sale in cans or bottles. Some beers are simply draft-only. The good news about these beers is you're more likely to have them fresh since they aren't hanging out in bottles on shelves.

How can I tell how old beer is?

That's a big question. Almost every brewer puts a date and time stamp on their beer packaging. On bottles, it's generally on the neck. On cans, it's on the bottom. Sometimes, it's printed on the label. To make things more confusing, sometimes the stamp uses an internal code. In these cases, you can typically find the code information on the brewery website's FAQ page.

How do I know what food goes best with what beer?

Great question! I will first state that no one – not even me! – can state categorically which food pairing is best for every beer. Everyone has different tastes. A good start toward thinking about how beer interacts with our palates is to read *Tasting Beer: An Insider's Guide to the World's Greatest Drink*. The author is

Randy Mosher, and the book has become a key resource for beer servers studying for the Cicerone test. It's also a damn fun read, and there's a whole chapter about pairing food with beer.

What's the nutritional value of craft beer?

I've got some bad news for you. No beer is really good for you. But just as there is a wide range of craft beer prices, there is a decent range of caloric damage, too. A super-light Session IPA, for example, will only be about 150 calories. That's about the same as a Coors Banquet Beer. Something like a Barrel-Aged Stout, though, will be closer to 400-600 calories. That's the equivalent of a six-inch meatball sub.

How do I find other people who are into craft beer?

There are quite a few sites that I've mentioned throughout this book that offer a venue for craft beer lovers, like BeerAdvocate and Untappd. There are also groups on social media. You can search for craft beer tasting groups on Facebook or Instagram. I also recommend bellying up to the bar at your local taproom or gastropub. I promise someone will bend your ear at some point!

About the Expert

Paul Deines is a beer and culture journalist from New York. His work has appeared in SR-Mag, Brew Studs, and Hop Culture. He has traveled the country, exploring the influence of the craft beer industry in America. This has put him in close contact with brewers, scientists, lobbyists, economists, advocates, and aficionados.

Paul also ghostwrites novels, crafts marketing copy, and writes video game dialogue. He is a produced playwright and director whose work has been performed on stages in New York, Boston, Florida, West Virginia, Indiana, and Kentucky.

You can find Paul's writing on film, theatre, art, politics, and, of course, beer at his personal website, The Curiograph (thecuriograph.com). You can follow him on Twitter at @thecuriograph.

HowExpert publishes quick 'how to' guides on all topics from A to Z by everyday experts. Visit HowExpert.com to learn more.

Recommended Resources

- HowExpert.com – Quick 'How To' Guides on All Topics from A to Z by Everyday Experts.
- HowExpert.com/free – Free HowExpert Email Newsletter.
- HowExpert.com/books – HowExpert Books
- HowExpert.com/courses – HowExpert Courses
- HowExpert.com/clothing – HowExpert Clothing
- HowExpert.com/membership – HowExpert Membership Site
- HowExpert.com/affiliates – HowExpert Affiliate Program
- HowExpert.com/jobs – HowExpert Jobs
- HowExpert.com/writers – Write About Your #1 Passion/Knowledge/Expertise & Become a HowExpert Author.
- HowExpert.com/resources – Additional HowExpert Recommended Resources
- YouTube.com/HowExpert – Subscribe to HowExpert YouTube.
- Instagram.com/HowExpert – Follow HowExpert on Instagram.
- Facebook.com/HowExpert – Follow HowExpert on Facebook.

www.ingramcontent.com/pod-product-compliance
Lightning Source LLC
LaVergne TN
LVHW091559060526
838200LV00036B/908